Contents

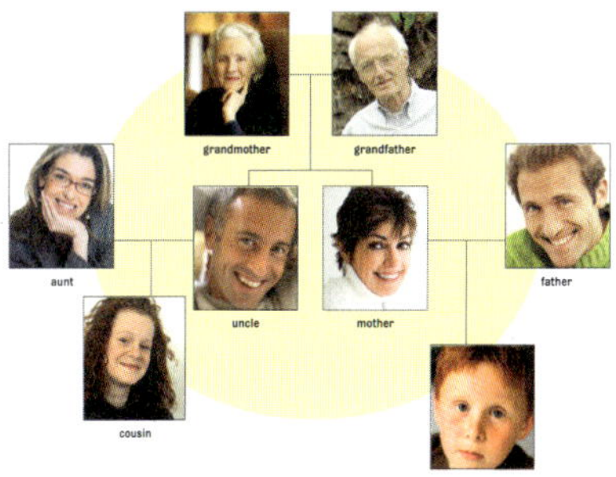
grandmother
grandfather
aunt
father
uncle
mother
cousin

UNIT 1 Welcome back

A song 4 U *Going places*

1/2 CD 1 MP3

1 Listen and sing.

At first I went to Paris.
I heard that it was great.
At first I went to Paris.
My plane was really late.
My room was very small,
three metres wall-to-wall.

Why did you go away?
Why did you not just stay –
at HOME?

Then I went to London.
I heard that it was cool.
Then I went to London.
Oh, I was such a fool.
I didn't like the food.
The weather was not good.

Why did you go away? …

Then I went to Lisbon.
It's nice there, people said.
Then I went to Lisbon.
I went there – and I fled.
Tourists everywhere.
What are they doing there?

Why did you go away? …

And now I'm home again,
but I am all alone.
I'm home, but no one's
calling me.
I'm sitting by the phone!

My flat's so small.
My friends are gone.
The weather isn't good.
I'd really like to go away.
I'd love to go on holiday!!

SbX

2 **Read Oliver's Internet project. Which information (A or B) is for boys and which is for girls?**

http://www.sanford.co.uk/oliver

Welcome to our world

Hi, my name's Oliver. I'm twelve years old. I go to Sanford school. It's in a small village in Scotland, about 20 miles from Glasgow. I'm in class 8B. There are ten girls and eight boys in our class. I asked them questions about how they spend their free time. Here are their answers.

1 What are your hobbies?
- **A** football (8), rugby (5), video games (8), swimming (2)
- **B** swimming (10), dancing (5), horse riding (5), gymnastics (1)

2 Where do you spend time with your friends?
- **A** in the park (8), at the cinema (3), at home (8)
- **B** at the cinema (10), in the town (5), in the park (8)

3 What is your favourite food?
- **A** chocolate (8), fish (6), chips (8), pizza (6)
- **B** chips (10), ice cream (6), chocolate (10), curry (6)

4 What are your favourite types of video game?
- **A** skateboarding (4), action and adventure (4)
- **B** *Harry Potter* (10), *Lara Croft* (2)

5 What do you buy with your pocket money?
- **A** sweets (6), video games (4), CDs (1)
- **B** sweets (8), jewellery (4), magazines (6)

6 What pets have you got?
- **A** dogs (6), hamsters (2), mice (4), cats (2)
- **B** dogs (5), guinea pigs (3), cats (4), horse (1)

7 What are your favourite TV programmes?
- **A** football (3), *Smallville* (5)
- **B** *The OC* (7), nature programmes (4)

3 **Look at 2 again. Write sentences about the things below. Use the words in the box.**

~~have got~~
has got
buys
like
have got

1 

Two boys have got hamsters.

2 

....

3 

....

4 

....

5 

....

Get talking Reporting

■ **4** **Work in groups of four. Ask the questions from the survey and note the answers. Report your answers to the class.**

> Four of us have got a cat. One of us has got a dog.

Vocabulary School subjects

3 CD 1 SbX ● **5** **Listen and number the school subjects. Say which subject you like best.**

4 Maths

2 English

9 Geography

10 History

7 Science

6 Music

5 Art

8 Information Technology (IT)

3 French

1 Design and Technology

11 Physical Education (PE)

4 CD 1 ● **6** **Here is Oliver's timetable. Listen and complete.**

	Monday	1 Thuesday	2 Wednesday	3 Tuesday	Friday
9 - 9.55 a.m.	English	Maths	Science	French	12 Sciens
10 - 10.55	4 French	English	8 History	Science	Information Technology
BREAK					
11.15 - 12.10	Design and Technology	6 Geo	Maths	10 DT	History
LUNCH					
1 - 1.55 p.m.	Maths	Science	9 PE	English	13 Maths
2 - 2.35	Art	French	PE	11 ART	English
2.40 - 3.15	5 Music	7 Histori	PE	Music	Geography

▶ WB pp. 4, 5, 6 ▶ CYBER HOMEWORK 1

5
CD 1
MP3
SbX

7 **Read the story. Then listen to it.**

First day at school

It was the first day of the new school year. All the kids were really excited. There were a lot of holiday stories to tell. Everyone wanted to talk.
The new teacher, Miss Cross, asked everyone to sit down and listen.
'OK,' she said. 'Who wants to tell me about their holidays?'
Twenty arms went up in the air.
'Let's start with Sara,' said Miss Cross.
We didn't hear any other stories in that lesson.
Sara's family always go somewhere exciting for their holiday. This year was the same.
'My family – that's me, my mum, my dad and my five-year-old brother Michael – went to Australia,' she said. 'We went to North Queensland. It was really beautiful and we had a great time swimming in the sea and playing on the beach.'
'Boring!' said Andrew Wilson.
'Sh!' said Miss Cross. Sara went on.
'One day, my brother was near the sea on his own. When he came back, he had a beautiful shell in his hand. He showed it to us.'
'So what?' said Andrew Wilson.
'Well, I saved my brother's life.'
'I don't believe you,' said one boy.
'How?' shouted another.
'My brother looked in the shell. He told us there was a strange blue and yellow thing inside. He started to put his fingers inside. He wanted to pull it out. Then I remembered about the blue ring octopus.'
'The what?' Andrew Wilson asked.
'The blue ring octopus – I read about it before we went. It lives in the sea, near Australia and Japan. It's small, but it's really poisonous. It can kill you with one bite. I hit my brother's hand and the shell fell onto the sand. Then we saw a small blue and yellow octopus come out of the shell. Of course, we didn't touch it.'
'We don't believe you,' said lots of the students.
'There's no octopus that's so dangerous,' said Andrew Wilson.
'There's one way to find out,' said Miss Cross. 'Let's check on the Internet!'

8 **Find the past tenses of these verbs in the text. Underline them and write them in your exercise book.**

be	tell	save	want	say	fall	ask	shout
see	read	go	hit	show	remember	come	have

■ **9** **Look at the webpage for the blue ring octopus. Was Sara telling the truth?**

The blue ring octopus is very dangerous. It lives in warm water off the coast of Australia, New Guinea, Indonesia and the Philippines. It lives for about two and a half years. The blue ring octopus has blue rings on its body and on its eight arms. It's about the size of a golf ball. It's dark yellow, but when you attack it, it turns bright yellow. The rings turn bright blue.
The blue ring octopus hunts during the day. It eats fish. It bites the fish and kills them with its poison. The blue ring octopus also uses the poison to kill attackers. The poison is so strong and dangerous that it can kill a man. There is no medicine against the poison.

■ **10** **Complete the questions with the question words in the box. Then write the answers to the questions.**

How
What
Where
When
How
What

1 .... does the blue ring octopus live?
2 .... long does it live?
3 .... many arms has it got?
4 .... colour is it?
5 .... does it hunt?
6 .... does it eat?

Writing *for your Portfolio*

11 **Write a short text about your summer holidays. See the examples below.**

● **Text 1**

This year my family stayed at home. I got up late every day. In the mornings I usually watched TV. After lunch I played volleyball or went swimming. In the evenings I played on my computer. I sometimes went to the cinema. It was the perfect holiday.

■ **Text 2**

I went to Italy with my family for two weeks. We spent one week in Rome and one week on the beach near Rome. In Rome we saw a lot of famous buildings and museums. It was very interesting, but I was very tired at the end.
The beach was great. I swam in the sea and played volleyball every day. I met a lot of nice Italian kids, but I didn't speak Italian. We spoke English! I loved my holidays.

WB p. 7

6 CD 1 MP3

12 **Read and listen to the poem.**

The furious octopus

The octopus, the octopus
is sometimes very furious.
You shake his first arm and you see
some octo-ink right on your knee.
You shake the others – two to eight –
and suddenly it's much too late
to get away.

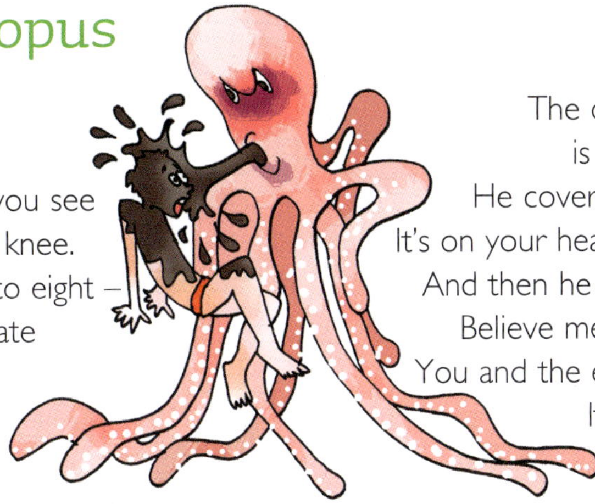

The octopus, the octopus
is getting really furious.
He covers you in ink so black.
It's on your head and legs and back.
And then he hugs you really tight.
Believe me, this is quite a sight:
You and the eight-armed octopus.
It's furious, so furious.

Grammar

SbX

Present simple (revision)

Du verwendest das *present simple*, um über Tatsachen zu sprechen.

The blue ring octopus **eats** fish.

When you **attack** it, it **turns** bright yellow. Where **does** the octopus **live?**

SbX

Past simple (revision)

Mit Hilfe des *past simple* berichtest du über Ereignisse und Situationen in der Vergangenheit.

Bei regelmäßigen Verben *(regular verbs)* hängst du ein *-ed* an das Verb:

play – We **played** on the beach. show – He **showed** it to us.

Einige Verben haben unregelmäßige Formen im *past simple*:

go – We **went** to Australia. read – I **read** about it before the holiday.

UNIT 2 Did we catch them?

Vocabulary

7 CD 1 SbX

1 **Look at the picture. Listen to the words. Then write the numbers in the right circles. How many words can you remember?**

1 stage
2 assistant
3 floor
4 hypnotist
5 hypnotise
6 medal
7 wallet
8 pick up

Time for a sketch

8 CD 1 MP3 SbX

2 **Listen and read.**

"Pronto!" – *A play*

The characters

Charles Granger, a hypnotist
Vivien Tate, his assistant
Roger Allen, a man at the show
Claire Grimes, his girlfriend
Inspector Lime
Sergeant Lewis
a doctor at the hospital

SCENE 1

A show with Charles, a hypnotist, on stage. With him is his assistant Vivien. In front of them there are tables with people sitting at them.

Charles And now, ladies and gentlemen, we need a man for a little experiment. What about you, sir?
Roger No, thank you.
Claire Oh, come on Roger. Maybe it's fun. Please do it.
Roger Oh, alright.
Charles Come up here, sir.

(Roger walks on stage. Applause)

What's your name?
Roger I'm Roger.

Charles Please have a seat, Roger. I'm going to hypnotise you. Look at this medal. I'm going to swing it. You follow it with your eyes – that's all.

Roger And then?

Charles And then I'm going to give you some commands. And you are going to do what I say.

Claire Tell him to do the washing-up every day!

(Laughter)

Charles Right, here we go. You only hear what I say. You only follow my commands.

(He hypnotises Roger)

Good! Stand up! Stand on one leg. Hop around. Very good. Jump down to your friend. Kiss her hand. Very good. Come back here again. Give me your watch Thank you, very good. When I say "Pronto" – you wake up again. You don't remember anything, of course! One, two, three – "Pronto".

Roger What happened? What did you do? Did you hypnotise me? What did I do?

Charles It's alright. You gave me your watch.

Roger I didn't. *(He checks.)* I did. Give it back to me.

Vivien Here you are, sir. Thank you, sir.

Charles Applause for the gentleman.

(Applause)

SCENE 2

After the show, Charles and Vivien are alone.

Vivien Did it work?

Charles Of course it did. I gave Roger the secret commands.

Vivien So, we're going to be rich?

Charles Very rich, baby, very rich.

Vivien Do you think he can break into the museum?

Charles Yes, he can. He's very strong.

Vivien Did you tell him to throw the jewels in the bushes?

Charles I did. We pick up the jewels. The police pick up Roger.

(They both laugh.)

SCENE 3

In a room of the museum.
In the background there is a broken window.
There is broken glass everywhere.

Inspector Lime	Come on, Lewis. Tell me the facts.
Sgt Lewis	Somebody broke into the museum, took the Deng Jewels and jumped out of the window.
Inspector Lime	Jumped out of the window? Why didn't he use the door?
Sgt Lewis	The alarm went off when he broke in and the security guards came.
Inspector Lime	I see. Any clues?
Sgt Lewis	Yes, we found blood under the window, but no thief.
Inspector Lime	Ah, what have we got here? A wallet!
Sgt Lewis	Don't touch it, sir.
Inspector Lime	But my hands are clean!
Sgt Lewis	I know, sir. But we need the fingerprints. The thief's fingerprints. Not yours!
Inspector Lime	Ah, yes. Hm, hm. Sorry, errm. And just look at all the mess around here.
Sgt Lewis	Don't walk around in it, sir.
Inspector Lime	You're right. My shoes are getting dirty.
Sgt Lewis	No, the footprints, sir.
Inspector Lime	Am I making footprints? Well, the museum people can clean them up.
Sgt Lewis	Not your footprints, sir. The thief's footprints. I have to go now, sir. See you at the station.
Inspector Lime	Yes, yes. Good man. Off you go.

SCENE 4

Sgt Lewis is at the door of Claire's house. She's talking to him.

Sgt Lewis I'm trying to find Mr Allen. I've got his wallet. This address was in it.

Claire Oh yes, he's my boyfriend.

Sgt Lewis I see. Can I talk to him?

Claire Is it about the accident? He's still in hospital. And he can't remember what happened.

Sgt Lewis An accident? Tell me more about it.

SCENE 5

In a room at the hospital.

Sgt Lewis Sir, can you hear me?

Claire He doesn't react.

Sgt Lewis Sir, please, talk to me. It's very important.

(The door opens, and a doctor comes in.)

Doctor What are you doing here? This man is in shock.

Sgt Lewis I'm from the police, sir.

Doctor I don't care. I want you out now. *Pronto!*

(Suddenly Roger sits up and starts walking stiffly towards the door.)

Doctor Hey, what's going on? Don't get out of bed!

Claire Oh, my God, you said "Pronto". That's what the hypnotist said.

Sgt Lewis The hypnotist? Tell me more.

SCENE 6

In Inspector Lime's office at the police station.

Inspector Lime Look at the paper, Lewis!

Sgt Lewis Why, sir?

Inspector Lime It says 'Inspector Lime solves another case! Jewels back at the museum.' Let me read it to you.

Sgt Lewis No, sir. Thank you, sir.

Inspector Lime Alright. I like that. 'Inspector Lime solves another case!' Where did you catch them, Lewis? The paper doesn't say.

Sgt Lewis The hypnotist and his friend were already on a plane to Singapore. I phoned the police in Singapore this morning and they arrested them an hour ago.

Inspector Lime Fantastic! We did an excellent job!

(He takes the newspaper.)

Inspector Lime 'Inspector Lime solves another case!' I like that!

The end

SbX

3 Circle Y *(Yes)* or N *(No)*.

1	Did Roger want to go on stage?	Y / N
2	Did Charles tell Roger to kiss Claire's hand?	Y / N
3	Did the hypnotist give Roger secret commands?	Y / N
4	Did Roger break into a bank?	Y / N
5	Did Sergeant Lewis find a wallet?	Y / N
6	Did the wallet belong to Claire?	Y / N
7	Did Sergeant Lewis go to see Claire?	Y / N
8	Did Roger wake up in hospital when he heard the word "hypnotist"?	Y / N
9	Did the police catch the thieves in England?	Y / N
10	Did Inspector Lime love the article in the paper?	Y / N

CYBER HOMEWORK 3
WB pp. 11, 12, 13

SbX

Grammar Past simple

Verneinung (*negation*)

The thief **didn't take** everything.
The inspector **didn't catch** the thief.
I **didn't do** it.

SbX

Fragen (*questions*)

Did you **hypnotise** me?
Did you **read** the newspaper?

Complete. Write *did* and *didn't*.

So bildest du die Verneinungen im *past simple:* Person + ... + *base form* des Verbs.
So bildest du Fragen im *past simple*: [2] .... + Person + *base form* des Verbs.

Wichtig: Kein *did* oder *didn't* mit *was, were* und *could!*
Roger **wasn't** at home.
Vivien and Charles **weren't** on a plane to Paris.
Sergeant Lewis **couldn't** talk to Roger.
Was Roger a thief?
Were Charles and Claire on their way to Singapore?

More irregular verbs

break – **broke**	find – **found**	take – **took**	catch – **caught**
give – **gave**	get – **got**	have – **had**	say – **said**

Get talking The past

4 Ask your partner about yesterday.

play do read go go help have watch

... your homework?
... to the cinema?
... TV?
... a book?
... your mum with the washing-up?
... a video game?
... for a run?
... a good time?

WB p. 14 CYBER HOMEWORK 4

The Story of the Stones 1 It's only a dream

1 Match the names to the characters.

1 Darkman
2 Sarah
3 Sunborn
4 Daniel
5 Emma

4 .... 5 .... 2 .... 1 .... 3 ....

2 Watch Episode 1 and complete the sentences with names from 1.

1 Darkman........ makes a promise.
2 Daniel........ has three dreams about Darkman.
3 Sarah........ dreamt she was on a rope.
4 Emma........ says they have to speak to Sunborn.
5 Daniel........ thinks Darkman is dead.

3 Write a message to Sunborn from the children.

....

....

....

....

Everyday English

4 Watch Episode 1 again. Complete the sentences.

I mean | Oh, come on | I promise

Daniel Yeah, let's get in touch with her.

Sarah 1 Oh, come on........ . They're only dreams.

Darkman I'll get them. 2 I promise........ .

Daniel It's the third time this week.

Sarah Me too. 3 I mean........, I have almost the same dream.

A Song 4 U *The Inspector Lime song*

9/10 CD 1

5 Listen and sing.

Did you see the broken door?
Were there footprints on the floor?
Did they really have a gun?
Did they drive off? Did they run?

Reporters here, reporters there,
reporters shouting everywhere.
Reporters here, reporters there,
reporters shouting everywhere.
Come on, let's call Inspector Lime.
He solves each case in record time.
Come on, let's call Inspector Lime.
He solves each case, he solves each case,
yes, he solves each case in record time.

Did they take the jewellery?
And the owner? Where was he?
Did they steal some money, too?
Were there three men or just two?

Reporters here, …

Writing *for your Portfolio*

■ **6 Complete the dialogue. (I = Inspector, W = Witness)**

I What [1] ……………………………………………?
W I saw a man with a large bag in his hands.
I What [2] …………………………………………… do?
W He threw the bag into the bush over there.
I And then?
W Then he walked away.
I [3] …………………………………… look nervous?
W No, [4] …………………………………… . He looked very calm.
I Why [5] ……………………… call the police then?

★ **7 Continue the conversation. Write four more sentences.**

UNIT 3 Oops!

SbX ● **1 Read the stories and then answer the questions.**

The cup-holder

Mr Custer bought a computer. It was a really good one with a DVD and a great flatscreen. After two weeks he phoned the computer shop. "I like my new computer very much," he said, "but I've got a real problem with it."
"What kind of computer have you got?" the shop assistant asked.
"The one with the cup-holder," said Mr Custer.
"I don't understand," the man at the shop said. "The one with the cup-holder?"
"Yeah, the cup-holder at the front of the computer doesn't work. It goes in and out and it spills my coffee."
The cup-holder was, in fact, the DVD-drive.

The wrong uncle

Mrs Browning and her husband were at Gatwick airport in London. They wanted to pick up Mrs Browning's uncle who was on a plane from New York. It was the first meeting between Mrs Browning and her uncle. Mrs Browning had a photo of her uncle in her hand. Suddenly, she said: "Look! It's that man over there!"
"Which man?" asked her husband.
"The one in the green coat!" answered his wife. Mrs Browning ran over to the man and kissed him. Then they took him to the car park, but the man didn't really want to go with them.
"Just get in the car! I'm sure you're tired from the long flight," said Mr Browning and pushed him into the car. When Mr Browning started the car, the man tried to jump out.
"Take my money," he said, "and let me go!"
Mr and Mrs Browning looked at the man.
"Please let me go! I must catch my flight to Paris!"
The man was not Mrs Browning's uncle, but a complete stranger!

1 What kind of computer did Mr Custer buy?
2 What did he do when he was not happy with it?
3 What problem did Mr Custer have with his computer?
4 What did Mr and Mrs Browning want to do at Gatwick airport?
5 Why did she believe the man in the green coat was her uncle?
6 Mrs Browning kissed the man. What happened then?

WB p. 17

11 CD 1

2 **Listen to the story *Modern Art* and circle T *(True)* or F *(False)*.**

1 Mrs Smith had a new job in a shop. T / F
2 The director came to check on Mrs Smith. T / F
3 The floor was still dirty. T / F
4 Part of the modern sculpture was missing. T / F
5 The jacket with five roses was missing. T / F
6 The jacket with the roses was part of a sculpture. T / F

3 **Think of the stories in 1 and 2 again. Who do you think said these sentences?**

1 What an old jacket!
2 I bought it in your shop two weeks ago.
3 What did you do with the roses?
4 I'm so happy to see you!
5 It's not a cup-holder, sir!
6 He looked like the man in the photo.

12 CD 1 MP3 SbX

4 **Listen to the dialogue and act it out.**

Richard	Dad?
Dad	What is it?
Richard	Can I have another T-shirt?
Dad	Why? What's wrong with the blue one?
Richard	Nothing, but I want my extra large one; the one that's got an alien on it.
Dad	Sorry, I can't give you that one.
Richard	Why not?
Dad	I put it into the washing-machine. And now it's extra small.
Richard	Oh, Dad!

WB p. 18 CYBER HOMEWORK 5

Time for a sketch

13 CD 1 MP3

5 **Listen and read.**

The fireman and the cat

Fire chief Did you do the job?
Fireman Yes, sir, we did.
Fire chief OK. What did the old lady say?
Fireman She cried, sir.
Fire chief Did she cry because she was happy?
Fireman Well, no. She was happy, but only at first.
Fire chief Why at first?
Fireman Well, sir, because we got the cat out of the tree …
Fire chief And?
Fireman And the lady was happy and invited us for tea.
Fire chief Right. So why did she cry? Explain, man.
Fireman Well, sir, we had tea and then I had a shock.
Fire chief Why did you have a shock?
Fireman Because the cat jumped on my back.
Fire chief But why did the lady cry?
Fireman Because I fell on the table and broke the teapot and all the cups!

Sounds right /w/

14 CD 1 MP3

6 **Listen and repeat.**

Why and why and why!
Why is it always why?
Why not ask me when,
or where or what or who?
It's something you could do.

Get talking Giving reasons

7 **Work in pairs. Talk to your partner about the following: a TV series, a school subject, a book, a CD. Make short dialogues. Use words from the box.**

exciting fun interesting cool funny great boring bad too long

A Do you like *Buffy?*
B Yes, I do.
A Why do you like it?
B Because it's exciting.

A Do you like *Buffy?*
B No, I don't.
A Why not?
B Because it isn't scary.

WB p. 19

Grammar *one / ones; why / because*

SbX

one / ones

Wenn du über gleiche Dinge sprichst, aber das Nomen nicht immer wiederholen möchtest, dann kannst du das Nomen durch *one* oder *ones* ersetzen.
'What kind of computer have you got?' 'I've got the **one** with the cup-holder.'

Complete with *one* or *ones*.

Du verwendest [1]..............., wenn du ein Nomen im *singular* nicht wiederholen willst.
Du verwendest [2]..............., wenn du ein Nomen im *plural* nicht wiederholen willst.

SbX

why / because

Why did you have a shock? – **Because** the cat jumped on my back.
Why did the lady cry? – **Because** I fell on the table, and broke the teapot and all the cups.

Writing *for your Portfolio*

8 Complete the dialogue. Then write a similar dialogue. Use *why* and *because*.

1 ......Why didn't you...... help to paint the room today?
I didn't help because I was tired.
2 ......Why are you...... tired?
I was tired because I didn't sleep much.
3 ......Why you didn't...... sleep much?
I didn't sleep much because I helped to paint the room yesterday.

UNIT 4 Halloween

Vocabulary Halloween

15 CD 1 SbX

1 **Look at the pictures and listen. Write the numbers next to the words.**

- ☐ "trick or treat"
- 1 ghost
- ☐ apple-bobbing
- ☐ a pumpkin
- ☐ a haunted house
- ☐ a vampire
- ☐ a witch

A Song 4 U *The Halloween Moon*

16/17 CD 1 MP3

2 **Listen and sing.**

It was twenty years ago,
three kids went to that house.
All of them went in.
None of them came out.
No one knows what happened
on that cold and windy night.
But everyone remembers
the moon was really bright.
The moon was really bright,
as bright as tonight.

The Halloween moon shines
on our little town
and the town goes crazy
till the moon goes down.

It was fifteen years ago
that Johnny went away.
We only found his hat
when we looked for him all day.
No one knows what happened
on that cold and windy night.
But everyone remembers
the moon was really bright.
The moon was really bright,
as bright as tonight.

The Halloween moon …

It's Halloween again.
It's midnight really soon.
I'm lost in these woods.
I can only see the moon.
No one will remember
what happened on this night.
But we will all remember
the moon was really bright.
The moon was really bright,
as bright as tonight.

The Halloween moon …

SbX

3 **Read the webpage. Then write the names under the pictures.**

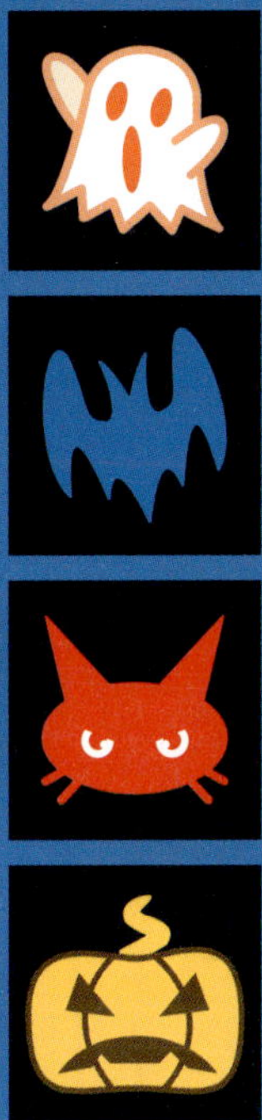

The question was: Do you have any Halloween traditions or fun things to do?
Your answers were:

George, USA, aged 11
My mum gets a scary film from the DVD shop. We change the house into a haunted castle and then we invite friends for a Halloween party. We eat popcorn and watch the film.

Megan, Ireland, aged 14
We always have a party. Everyone wears a mask. We're vampires, witches and ghosts. And we also play 'bobbing the apple'. There are lots of apples in water and you try to take them out with your mouth. You can't use your hands. It's difficult but fun.

Steve, UK, aged 12
Me and my brothers usually go 'Trick or treating' with friends. We knock on people's doors and say 'Trick or treat'. People sometimes give us a treat; sweets, etc. But if they don't, we play a trick on them.

Henry, Canada, aged 11
Every year we take a pumpkin to school. We cut off the top and take out everything inside. Then we cut a scary face in it. Finally, we put a candle inside the pumpkin.

a

....

b

....

c

....

d

....

WB p. 23

Story time

18 CD 1 MP3 SbX

4 **Read the story. Then listen to it.**

Trick or treat

Last Halloween I went to play "Trick or treat" with my twin sister Kerry. "Larry and Kerry, don't go too far away," our mother said. But we didn't listen and soon we were on the other side of town. There we met a boy about the same age as us. He told us his name was Jim. He said he wanted to do "Trick or treat" with us. "There are some really good houses in this street," he told us. So we went with him.

At the end of the street was a really big old house with a big gate and a long drive up to the front door. We stopped and looked at it. It was the kind of house you see in horror films. "Let's try this house," said Jim. "We shouldn't go in there," I said. "And you shouldn't be a baby," said Jim. "Come on."

Jim walked up the long drive. We followed. An old man opened the door. He wasn't very happy to see us. "Trick or treat?" Jim said. The old man looked at us. "Go away," he said. "Go away – now!" He closed the door. "Come on," I said. And we walked to the gate. At the gate Jim stopped. "That man was mean," he said. "We should play a mean trick on him." "OK," I said. "Let's make ghost noises." "No," said Jim. "We should play a really mean trick on him." "Let's throw a stone at his window," said Kerry. "No," said Jim. "Let's put superglue in his door lock." "I think we should go home," I said. But it was too late.

Get talking

5 **Work in pairs. Think of an ending to the story.**

19 CD 1

6 **Now listen to the ending of the story.**

WB p. 24 CYBER HOMEWORK 7

7 **Put the sentences in the correct order.**

- [ ] They went to the other side of town.
- [ ] The old man shut the door on them.
- [ ] Jim showed them a big old house.
- [ ] The door of the house opened again.
- [ ] Jim disappeared.
- [1] Larry and Kerry went 'Trick or treating'.
- [ ] They met Jim.
- [ ] They knocked on the door.
- [ ] Larry and Kerry called the police.
- [ ] An old man opened the door.
- [ ] Jim went to put superglue in the lock.

8 **Complete the list of suggestions for "Trick or treat". Write *should* or *shouldn't*.**

1 You .... wear a Halloween costume.
2 You .... play really mean tricks on people.
3 You .... wear black clothes at night.
4 You .... take a bag with you for the sweets.
5 You .... always go with friends.
6 You .... stay out very late.
7 You .... go on your own.
8 You .... always tell an adult where you are going.

Sounds right *should – shouldn't*

20 CD 1

9 **Listen and check. Then say the sentences in 8 yourself.**

Writing *for your Portfolio*

10 **What should you do to have a great Halloween party?**
Write some sentences. Use the pictures to help you.
Then add three sentences starting with "*You shouldn't …* ".

buy...

wear...

have...

Example:
You shouldn't come late.

WB p. 25

The Story of the Stones 2 We're all in danger

1 Look at the pictures from Episode 1 and put them in order.

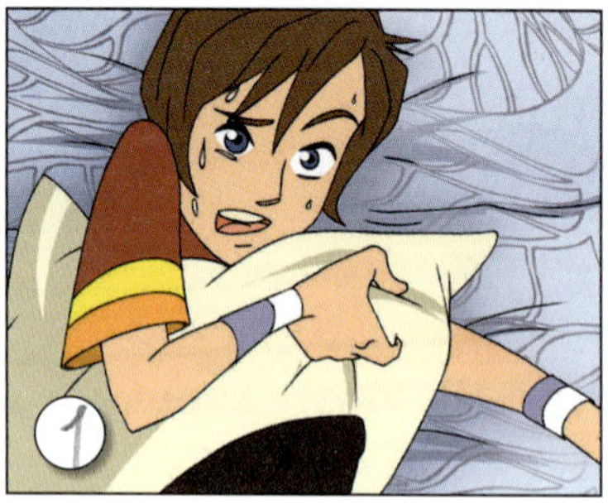

2 Can you remember who morphs into each of these animals? Write the names.

Daniel .... Emma .... Sarah ....

3 Watch Episode 2 and answer the questions.

1 Who is Darkman's master?
a) The Black Knight b) Demon Eyes c) The Lord of the Fire
2 What does Darkman's master want?
a) The belt and stones b) A spaceship c) The three stones
3 Which Lord wanted all the stones?
a) The Lord of the Earth b) The Lord of the Fire c) The Lord of the Water
4 Who is trying to find the stones?
a) Sunborn b) Darkman c) The Lords

Everyday English

4 Watch Episode 2 again. Complete the sentences and match them with the person who said them.

Here you are | get it | Something's wrong

1 Emma [1] Something's wrong .... It's two against one ...
2 Sarah [3] Only your stones can protect you now. Here you are ....
3 Sunborn [2] I still don't get it .... Why didn't Darkman die?

21 CD 1 MP3

11 Read and listen to the poem.

I'm not so keen on Halloween

I'm not so keen
on Halloween.
When my friends meet
for 'Trick or treat',
I'm not the one
who thinks it's fun
to run around
as witch or ghost.

What scares me most
is other kids
who hunt for treats,
who look for sweets.
They don't play tricks
but just give kicks
to get their treats,
to get your sweets.

Grammar *should, shouldn't*

SbX

Lies die Beispielsätze.

We **should go** home – it's late.
We **shouldn't go** in there – it's dangerous.
What **should** I **do**?

Complete the sentences with *should* or *shouldn't*.

Wenn du sagen willst, was jemand tun sollte, dann verwendest du [1]....................
Wenn du sagen willst, was jemand nicht tun sollte, dann verwendest du [2]....................
Wenn du um Rat fragst, dann verwendest du ebenfalls [3]....................
Bildung: *should/shouldn't* + *base form* (Nennform) des Zeitwortes.

1 **Read the text.**

Saved by a pig

August 5th, 2004 was a hot day in Worcester. Judith Crowe, her 5-year-old son Jeff and their little pig Bacon went swimming in the river near their home. Bacon was a very good swimmer. In fact, he was better than Jeff.
Judith and her son played and swam in the water for an hour. All the time Bacon was with them. Then Jeff's mother got out of the water to get a towel. "Stay here for a minute," she said. When she turned round, she saw Jeff in the middle of the river. The water was deeper and more dangerous there. He was in trouble.
Jeff's mother jumped into the water and started to swim. But Bacon was faster than Judith and got to the boy first.
The little boy put his arms around the pig. But he was bigger than the pig and he was heavier. The boy and the pig both disappeared under the water.
Jeff's mother didn't know what to do. Then suddenly she saw the little pig again. Jeff was on the pig's back. Her son was safe.

2 **Find the three incorrect sentences and correct them.**

1 It was a hot day in Worcester.
2 Jeff was 5 years old.
3 They went swimming in the sea.
4 They played and swam for two hours.
5 Judith got out of the water to get a drink.
6 The pig and Jeff disappeared under the water.

SbX

Grammar Comparatives

Wenn du zwei Dinge vergleichst, die verschieden sind, dann verwendest du das Wort *than*. An die englischen Eigenschaftswörter mit einer Silbe (*fast/slow/deep/old/*usw.) hängst du *-er* an.
He's old**er than** me.
She's fast**er than** me.

Bei manchen Eigenschaftwörtern verändert sich jedoch die Rechtschreibung: *hot / big / fat*, etc. – It's hott**er** today than yesterday.

heavy / angry / hungry, etc. –
Joe's heav**ier than** me.

An die englischen Eigenschaftswörter mit zwei Silben, die auf *-y*, *-le* und *-ow* enden (*happy, simple*) hängst du ebenfalls *-er* an.

Wenn das Eigenschaftswort mehr als zwei Silben hat, dann verwendest du *more* + *adjective* (*dangerous / difficult / interesting*, usw.).
The book is **more interesting than** the film.

Ausnahmen:
good – **better**
He was **better than** Jeff.
bad – **worse**
I'm bad at football, but he's **worse than** me!

WB p. 29

3 **Look back at the story. Ask and answer questions in pairs.**

1 Why did Judith and Jeff go swimming?
2 Why did Jeff's mother get out of the water?
3 Why was the water more dangerous in the middle?
4 Why did Bacon arrive at the boy first?
5 Why did the boy and the pig disappear under the water?

Vocabulary Adjectives

SbX **4** **Match the pictures with the adjectives. Write the numbers.**

1 small | 2 strong | 3 hairy | 4 clever | 5 heavy | 6 big | 7 dangerous

Get talking A guessing game

5 **Choose one of the animals. Make sentences using comparatives. Your partner guesses what animal it is. Use the words in the box in 4 to help you.**

a

b

c

d

e

f

g

h

A It's bigger than a mouse.
B Is it a guinea pig?
A No, it's heavier than a guinea pig.
B Is it a rabbit?
A That's right.

SbX

6 Read the gaming cards for these animals from Atlantis.

ANIMALS OF ATLANTIS
THE RUCKLE
The Ruckle was very exotic. It was half land animal and half bird but it didn't fly. It was as big as a rabbit. It was very friendly and many Atlantians had them for pets.

ANIMALS OF ATLANTIS
THE BUGBOY
The Bugboy was a small reptile. It was as small as a mouse but it was as dangerous as a snake. In fact, it was as poisonous as a blue ring octopus. Every year, hundreds of people died from its bite.

ANIMALS OF ATLANTIS
THE SNAPKLE
The Snapkle was a kind of dragon. It lived in the mountains outside of Atlantis. It was as big as an elephant. But it wasn't as beautiful as an elephant. In fact, it was very ugly.

7 Read the cards again and circle T *(True)* or F *(False)*.

1	Atlantians had Ruckles in their homes.	T / F
2	The Hipcop was friendlier than the Ruckle.	T / F
3	The Snapkle was bigger than an elephant.	T / F
4	The Bugboy was a kind of octopus.	T / F
5	The Hipcop wasn't as clever as a chimpanzee.	T / F
6	The Bugboy wasn't very dangerous.	T / F
7	The Ruckle was bigger than a rabbit.	T / F
8	The Snapkle was a beautiful animal.	T / F

ANIMALS OF ATLANTIS
THE HIPCOP
The Hipcop wasn't as friendly as the Ruckle but it was also a popular pet. It was as clever as a chimpanzee.

SbX

Grammar *as … as*

Wenn du sagen willst, dass zwei Dinge (Tiere, Personen) gleich groß, klein usw. sind, dann verwendest du *as … as*
It was **as** small **as** a mouse.
It was **as** dangerous **as** a snake.

Wenn du sagen willst, dass ein Ding (Tier, Person) nicht so (groß, klein usw.) ist wie ein(e) andere(s) Ding (Tier, Person), dann verwendest du *not as … as*
It was**n't as** friendly **as** the Ruckle.

Sounds right /dʒ/ /tʃ/

22 CD 1 MP3

8 Listen and repeat.

His name's Jim,
I'm more beautiful than him.
He's a chimpanzee,
and he's as big as me.

WB pp. 30, 31 CYBER HOMEWORK 9

23 CD 1

9 **Read the magazine article. Can you complete it with the missing numbers? Then listen and check.**

150 2 8 3 110 1 3

The most Amazing Animals in the world

The Estuarine crocodiles of Southeast Asia are the longest crocodiles in the world. They can be 1........ m long – as long as two cars together!

The bumblebee bat from Thailand is the smallest mammal in the world. It is 4........ cm long and weighs 5........ grams.

The world's most poisonous snake is the taipan. It lives in the deserts of Australia. It can be more than 2........ metres long.

The most dangerous animal in the world is the mosquito. It can carry malaria. Every year more than 6........ million people worldwide die from malaria.

The biggest animal on land or in the sea is the blue whale. It's also the heaviest. It weighs 3........ tons.

The fastest land animal in the world is the cheetah. It can run very fast – more than 7........ km/h.

SbX

Grammar Superlatives

Wenn du ausdrücken willst, dass etwas am größten, schwersten, schnellsten usw. ist, hängst du *-est* an das Adjektiv an:
fast / slow / deep / old, etc. – The cheetah is **the** fast**est** mammal in the world.

Bei einigen Adjektiven ändert sich die Schreibung:
hot / big / fat, etc. – The blue whale is **the** bigg**est** animal in the world.
heavy / angry / hungry, etc. – The blue whale is **the** heavi**est** animal in the world.

Bei Adjektiven, die aus drei oder mehr Silben bestehen, verwendest du *the most* + Adjektiv:
dangerous / interesting, etc. – The mosquito is **the most dangerous** animal in the world.

Ausnahmen:

good – **the best** She's **the best** player in the team.
bad – **the worst** It's **the worst** restaurant in town.

WB p. 32

10 **Whose eye is it? Match the eyes and the animals.**

1 ostrich
2 rhino
3 antelope
4 dolphin
5 chimpanzee
6 giraffe

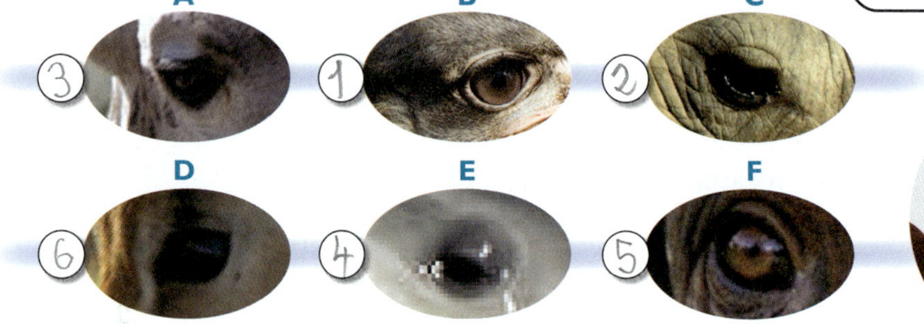

I think letter …
is the ostrich's eye.

24 CD 1 **11** **Listen and check.**

Get talking About animals

12 **Put the animals in order. Write 1, 2 and 3 in the boxes.**

The animal quiz

ANIMALS

1 Which is the tallest?
a [1] a giraffe
b [2] an ostrich
c [3] an elephant

2 Which is the longest?
a [2] an anaconda
b [1] a whale shark
c [3] a crocodile

3 Which is the fastest?
a [1] an antelope
b [3] a lion
c [2] a rabbit

4 Which is the most intelligent?
a [2] a dolphin
b [3] a pig
c [1] a chimpanzee

5 Which is the heaviest?
a [1] a blue whale
b [2] an elephant
c [3] a rhino

A I think the elephant is the tallest.

B I don't think so. I think the …

25 CD 1 **13** **Listen and check.**

CYBER HOMEWORK 10

A Song 4 U *A mouth as big as a house*

26/27 CD 1 MP3

14 **Listen and sing.**

Watch out everyone! Here comes Swift,
the friendliest shark in the sea.
He's got big teeth, but doesn't like meat.
He only eats pizza and only drinks tea.
He's always got a smile for you.
He's the friendliest shark in the sea.

Watch out everyone! Here comes Big Mouth,
the hungriest shark in the sea.
She's got a mouth as big as a house.
There's room in her tummy for you and me.
Be very careful. Don't swim close.
She's the hungriest shark in the sea.

Writing *for your Portfolio*

SbX

15 **Read about the Huffump.**

The Huffump was a kind of shark. It lived in the sea around Atlantis. It was as big as a whale and it was very dangerous. It had a really big mouth and more than 4,000 teeth. Every year it killed and ate more than 200 Atlantians. The Atlantians were very scared to swim in the sea.

16 **Now do the writing tasks.**

Design your own animal from Atlantis. Make up a name for the creature and write a text about it.

Kids in NYC 1

Homework first

Before you watch

1 Write the words under the pictures.

bedroom
living room
hall
kitchen

1.................. 2.................. 3.................. 4..................

2 What order do you think these pictures come in the DVD? Write 1–4.

A

B

C

D

Watch the story

3 Check your answers to 2.

4 Complete the sentences.

1 Steve is in the ....
2 Steve and Jenny want ....
3 Steve hasn't ....
4 Jenny did the geography ....
5 Jenny wants to ring her sister to ....

5 Complete the dialogue.

need
see
listen
want
remember
get
do
think

Jenny Clare? Hi, it's me. 1 ...., can you 2 ...... me a favor?
Clare It depends. What do you 3 .... ?
Jenny I 4 .... my Geography homework – it's in my school bag. Can you 5 .... it?
Clare Where is it?
Jenny In my room. I 6 ....
Clare Hang on then. Jenny? I'm in your room, but I don't 7 .... your bag.
Jenny I'm really sorry Clare, but I 8 .... now – I left it in the kitchen.

6 Answer the questions.

1 Where's Jenny's Geography homework? ....
2 Does Clare find the bag in the bedroom? ....
3 Where does Clare find the bag? ....
4 Why does Steve say 'This isn't right'? ....

Everyday English

7 Complete the dialogues.

It depends
Ready?
Can you do me a favour?
Hang on

Note:
favor = American English
favour = British English

Progress Check Units 1–5

Listening

28 CD 1

Listen to the dialogues and write the names of the dogs under the pictures.

Fifi Rover Spot Buddy Lady

1 .... 2 .... 3 .... 4 .... 5 ....

☐ 5

Reading

Read the story and tick the correct pictures.

The experiment

I was in my science class. The teacher asked us to do an experiment. He told us to listen very carefully. He told us to take the blue stone and put it in the red water and watch what happened. Then he told us to drink the water.
I went to the table where the stones were. I looked at them and took the biggest one. Then I went to the table where the water was. I looked at the bottles and took the green one.
I went back to my table and put the stone in the water. Nothing happened. "OK", I thought. "This isn't very exciting. Let's see what happens when I drink it." I drank it. Nothing happened. It was like water. "What a silly experiment." I thought.
I turned to ask my friend a question. He looked at me and laughed. Then another boy looked at me and started laughing too. Soon everyone in the class was laughing. The teacher too! Then I saw my face in the window. I was really hairy. I looked like a monster!

1 What lesson was it?

2 Which stone did the boy take?

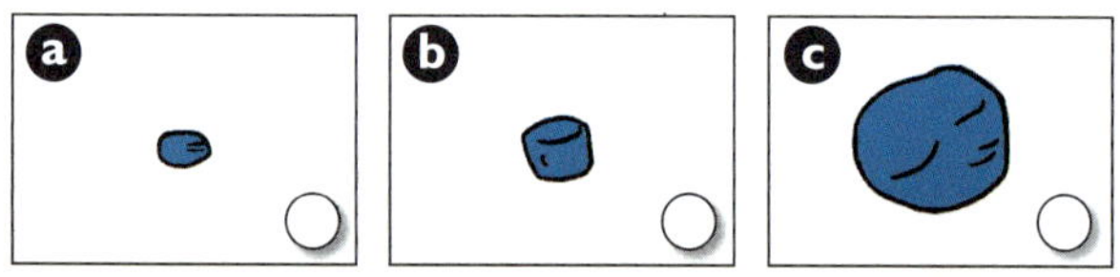

3 Which water did the boy take?

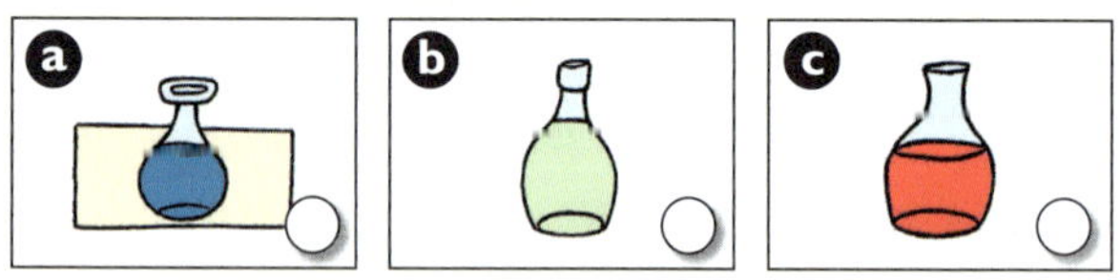

4 What happened when the boy put the stone in the water?

5 What did the boy see in the window?

☐ 5

Grammar

Circle the correct answer.

1 Where *do / does* he play football?
2 I didn't *break / broke* the window.
3 She's the *most / more* intelligent person I know.
4 I didn't do my homework *why / because* I was very tired.
5 If you feel ill you *should / shouldn't* go to bed.
6 It's *hottest / hotter* today than it was yesterday.
7 Who did you *give / gave* it to?
8 Don't wear your new shoes. Wear your old *one / ones*.
9 I'm scared. We should *go / to go* home.
10 The book's not as *good / better* as the film.

☐ 10

Vocabulary

Choose words in the box to answer the questions. There are four you do not need.

vampire
hairy
History
Maths
strong
dangerous
ghost
pumpkin
IT
Geography

1 Which school subject teaches you about the different countries in the world? ....
2 Which school subject teaches you about computers and how to use them? ....
3 What's "Kürbis" in English? ....
4 Which school subject teaches you about numbers and how to use them? ....
5 Which school subject teaches you about what happened in the past? ....
6 **A** Don't cross the street here!
B Why not?
A It's ....

☐ 6

Dialogue

Complete the dialogue with the words in the box. There are two words you do not need.

these did why ones should because those

Mum [1] .... you have a good time shopping?
Janet Yeah. I had fun.
Mum Did you buy [2] .... blue shoes you liked?
Janet No, I didn't. I bought the red [3] ....
Mum Really? [4] .... ?
Janet [5] .... they didn't have the blue shoes in my size.

☐ 5

How did you do?

Listening		
☺ 4-5	😐 2-3	☹ 0-1

Reading		
☺ 4-5	😐 2-3	☹ 0-1

Grammar		
☺ 7-10	😐 4-6	☹ 0-3

Vocabulary		
☺ 5-6	😐 3-4	☹ 0-2

Dialogue		
☺ 4-5	😐 2-3	☹ 0-1

Total		
☺ 25-31	😐 12-24	☹ 0-11

UNIT 6 Where's the post office?

Vocabulary Directions

29 CD 1 SbX

1 Gretta the witch is explaining to Sir Florestan, a knight, how to get to the dragon's place. Listen and follow the way. Write *D* where the dragon lives.

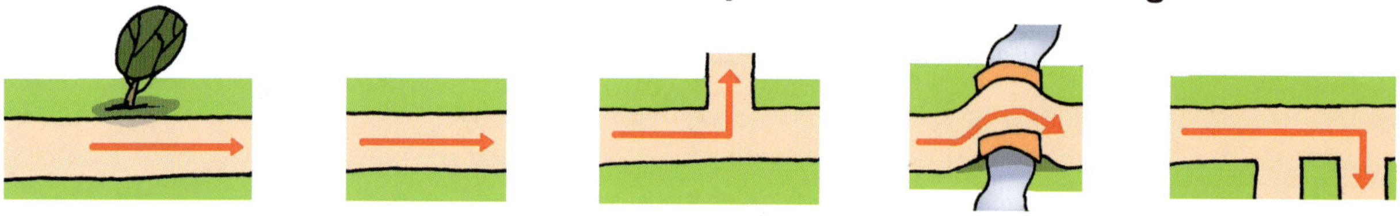

go past the tree | go straight ahead | turn left | cross the bridge | take the second right

Vocabulary Buildings

30 CD 1 SbX

2 **Match the words and the pictures. Then listen and check.**

1 railway station	12 police station	5 chemist's	3 post office	7 tourist office
10 bank	2 church	4 hospital	9 cinema	6 restaurant
8 music shop	11 supermarket			

3 **Read the dialogues and draw two of the missing signs where they belong.**

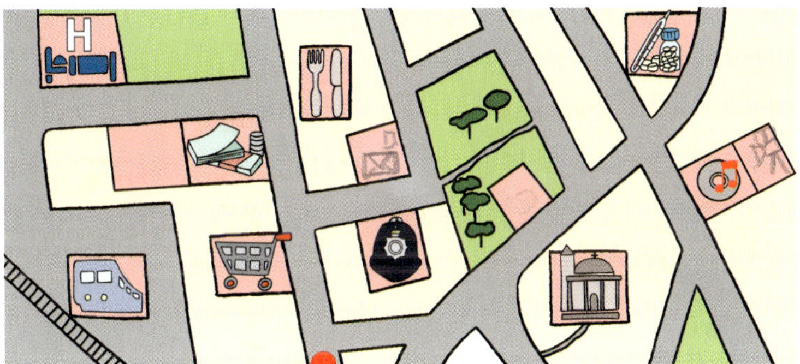

DIALOGUE 1

Woman	Excuse me, where's the post office?
Man	That's easy. You follow that road as far as the supermarket.
Woman	Alright. And then?
Man	Go past the supermarket and then turn left. On the corner of the next street, there's a large bank. And next to the bank there's the post office.
Woman	Thank you.
Man	You're welcome.

DIALOGUE 2

Boy	Excuse me.
Woman	Yes, dear?
Boy	Can you tell me where the Odeon cinema is?
Woman	The Odeon? Well, let me think. It's in Hill Road.
Boy	How do I get there?
Woman	Go straight on, take the second on the right and go past the police station.
Boy	OK, past the police station …
Woman	Then there's a little park in front of you. Go through the park. Turn right, then left, and then right again. The cinema is behind the large music shop.
Boy	Thank you.
Woman	Not at all.

31 CD 1

4 **Listen to two more dialogues and draw the other two signs on the map.**

WB pp. 36, 37

Get talking Giving directions

SbX

5 **Work in pairs. Partner A works with the map here, partner B works with the map in the Workbook (page 38).**

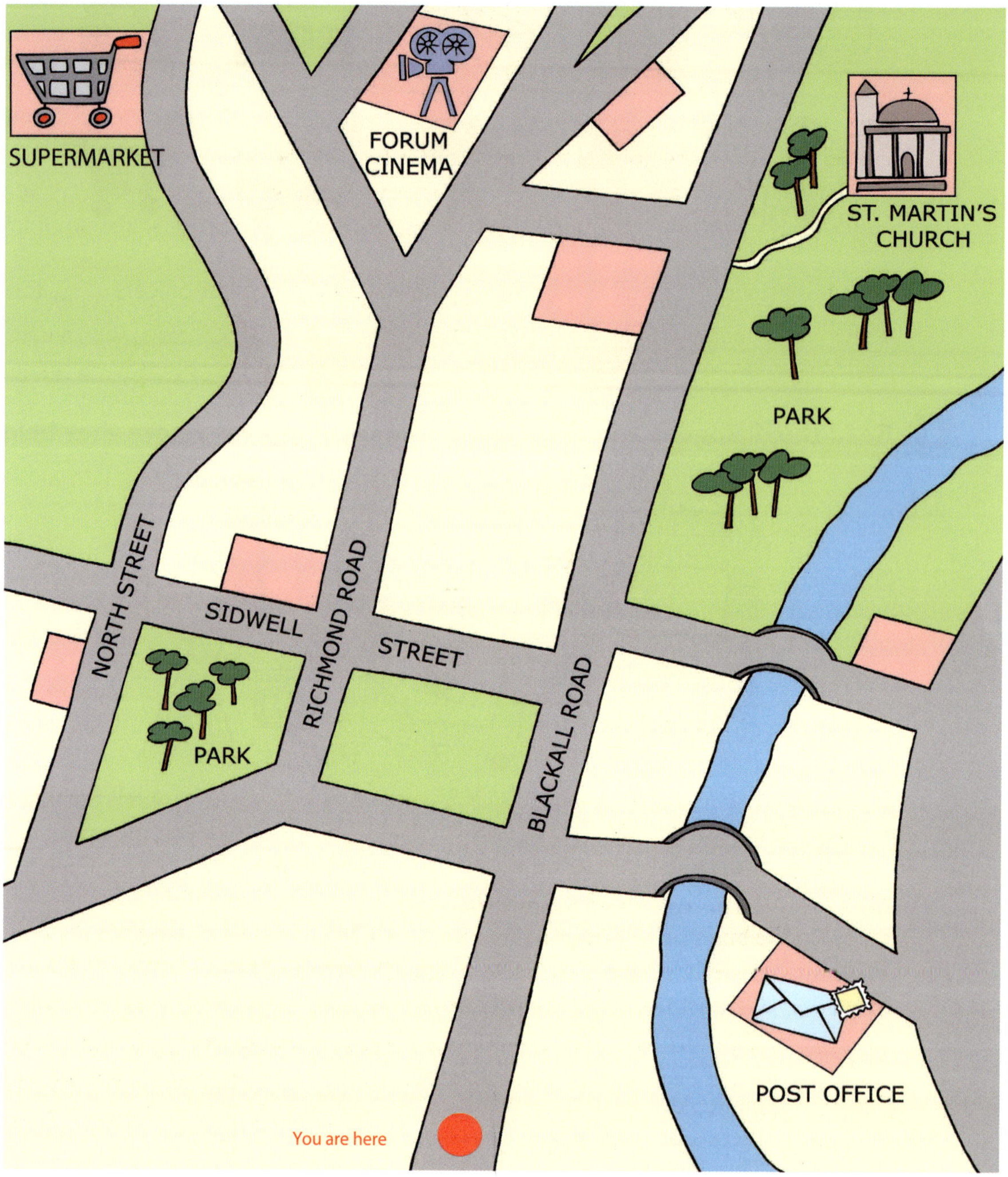

You ask your partner the way to the tourist office, the restaurant, the police station, the bank.

A Excuse me, how do I get to the tourist office? (Excuse me, I'm trying to find … / Excuse me, I'm looking for …)

B That's easy. Take the …

WB p. 38 CYBER HOMEWORK 11

Story time

32 CD 1 MP3 SbX

6 **Read the story. Then listen to it.**

Looking for Danielle

Last year a French girl stayed at our place. Her name was Danielle, and she was here with her classmates and her English teacher.
Danielle was not very good at finding her way. So Dad took her everywhere in the car. One day he had no time. He asked me to meet Danielle at the bus stop in Green Street, but I forgot.
I was in my room when the phone rang. It was Danielle. "Hallo, hallo," she said, "I'm lost. I don't know where I am. Can you help me?"

I was in trouble! I could hear my dad saying, "What did I tell you, George? Go and get Danielle from the bus stop in Green Street! No computer games for the rest of the week!"
"Of course!" I said. "Where are you?"
"I don't know," she said. "There are a lot of grey houses, and they all look the same. And there's a bus stop at the end of the road."
"Danielle," I said. "Listen. What's the name of the street?"
"I don't know. I can't see a street sign."
"Walk to the end of the road, Danielle," I said. "There's a sign."
"Ah yes, I can see it. Hallo? My battery's low."
"Danielle," I shouted. "Just tell me the name of the street. And stay where you are!"
"Ah yes, the name of the street is very long. It's … "
Just then there was a 'click'. I couldn't believe it!
I put on my jacket and got my bike. I thought: "She got off the bus in Green Street. So maybe she walked down the main road from there."
I went to the bus stop in Green Street and then followed the main road. Half an hour later – still no Danielle. I rode my bike back home. I went up and down some smaller roads – no Danielle.
Two hundred metres away from our house, there's a road up a long hill. I didn't want to go up that road, but then I thought, "OK, for five minutes … " I turned into the road. Then I checked out the side roads. First left – nothing. Second, third, fourth left – nothing. I was *sooo* tired. First right – and just 100 metres away, there was Danielle.

7 **Match the sentence halves.**

1 Danielle couldn't find her way
2 The phone call stopped because
3 George didn't know
4 George looked for
5 He found her only

[4] her on his bike.
[5] 300 metres away from their house.
[2] the battery of her mobile was low.
[3] where Danielle was.
[1] home from the bus stop.

A Song 4 U *Looking for Liz*

33/34 CD 1 MP3

8 **Listen and sing.**

I'm looking for my girlfriend.
I don't know where she is.
I'm looking for my girlfriend.
She's blonde. Her name is Liz.

Excuse me, sir.
Did you see her?
Where did she go?
I have to know.

She went along the High Street
and turned right at the shop.
She went as far as
Flower Square
and there I saw her stop.

I'm looking for my girlfriend.
I don't know where she is.
I'm looking for my girlfriend.
She's blonde. Her name is Liz.

Excuse me, sir …

I saw her stop at Flower Square.
I saw a young man wait for her.
They talked. They laughed.
They said goodbye.

Can I still catch her?
You can try.

9 **Put the dialogue in the correct order. Compare with your partner. Then act it out.**

5	**Jasmine**	The Carlton? The film's at the Odeon. Hurry up!
3	**Jasmine**	I'm in front of the cinema, too. The Odeon cinema.
1	**Jasmine**	Hey, Ron, where are you?
7	**Jasmine**	Go up Broad Street and turn left after the bank.
6	**Ron**	What's the quickest way?
2	**Ron**	I'm in front of the cinema.
8	**Ron**	Right. See you in five minutes.
4	**Ron**	Oh dear. Wrong cinema. I'm in front of the Carlton cinema.

Writing *for your Portfolio*

● **10** **Your friend is coming to visit you.**
Send an email with directions to your house.

Hi Bob,
This is how you get from the station to my house. From the station first go straight on. Then take the first street on the right. That's Hill Street. Go down Hill Street for about 150 metres, then turn left. Go straight ahead.
At the bank turn right, go past the post office, take the second left and you're in my street, Bristol Road. I live at number 34.
Love, Susan

SbX

Grammar Directions (Prepositions of place)

So sagst du jemandem, wie er/sie an ein bestimmtes Ziel gelangen kann.

Go straight ahead.
Take the first left / second right.
Go past the post office.

So sagst du jemandem, wo ein bestimmtes Ziel zu finden ist.
The cinema is **behind** the large shopping centre.
Next to the bank, there's the post office.
The restaurant is **opposite** the church.
There's a little park **in front of** you.
On the corner of the next street, there's a large bank.
It's just **round the corner**, beside the bank.

opposite

round the corner

in front of

WB p. 39
CYBER HOMEWORK 12

UNIT 7 Outdoor adventure

Vocabulary Places

CD 2 1 SbX

1 Listen and fill in numbers.

[11] hill	[10] stars	[9] valley	[15] sea	[3] motorway	[5] town	[7] forest	[14] sun
[6] fields	[1] mountain	[2] road	[16] village	[12] lake	[4] river	[8] moon	[13] beach

2 Work in pairs. Look at the picture for half a minute. One of you closes the book. Ask and answer questions.

You				Your partner
			village?	On the right-hand side.
			sea?	On the left-hand side.
Where	's		lake?	In the middle.
	are	the	…	In the top right-hand corner.
			fields?	In the bottom left-hand corner.
			…	Next to the …

WB p. 42

Get talking Making plans

3 **Listen and complete the dialogue.**

CD 2 · SbX

A Let's [1] go canoeing on Monday.
B Canoeing? I'm not sure.
A Well, you don't have to come along. I'll go alone, then.
B Wait a minute. I think I'll join you.
A Great. But bring [2] wormclows ! And you have to [3] wear a life jacket in the boat all the time.
B Of course. I know that.

Build a tree house!
When: Thursday 3 p.m.
Don't be late!
Get a hard hat from the office before you leave!

Go for a picnic!
When: Sunday 12 a.m.
Bring your own food and drink!
Clean up the picnic area after the picnic!

Go rock climbing!
When: Friday 11 a.m.
Bring warm clothes and good shoes.
Read the camp guide carefully.

Visit the waterfalls!
When: Saturday 2 p.m.
Don't be late!
Wear an anorak near the waterfalls.

4 **Work in pairs. Look at the notices above and act out dialogues.**

A Let's (visit/go/build) ....
B .... I'm not ....
A Well, you don't ....
B Wait ....
A Great. But .... And you ....

Sounds right *have to*

5 **Listen and repeat.**

CD 2 · MP3

A I can't stay here, I have to go.
B You have to go? But why?
A I have to move to London!
B I have to say 'goodbye'.

6 **Listen to Emma and Harry talking about a treasure hunt. Take notes in your exercise book, in a table like this one.**

CD 2

	When?	What did you find?	Where did you find it?
Emma			
Harry			

WB p. 43 · CYBER HOMEWORK 13

Story time

5 CD 2 MP3 SbX

7 **Read the story. Then listen to it.**

Treasure hunt

When Dad said that Gillie and I could go to an adventure holiday camp, I wasn't too excited. I didn't want to go to a holiday camp with my twelve-year-old sister! But Gillie really loved the idea. So I couldn't say no. But the camp was great! Lots of new friends and Gillie was OK too (most of the time ☺).

What I liked most about the camp were the surprise activities: wild water canoeing, rock climbing, a visit to the waterfall – these things were never boring! No wonder – Rick, Pamela, Laura, Jack and Ron (our guides) were fantastic. Especially Ron! He was really cool.

One Friday Gillie was very excited: "Chris, come quickly, there's a geo-caching treasure hunt with Ron tomorrow. Quick, only 20 kids can go!" 'Geo-caching???' I thought. I had no idea what it was – but I didn't want to ask. I was fourteen. And she was twelve, you know! "Geo-caching? Not a bad idea," I said. When we wrote our names on the list, I saw this note:

I went to speak to Ron later to find out more about geo-caching and this was what I learnt: for geo-caching you need a GPS unit. The camp guides tell you where you can find the 'treasure'. But they don't say things like "go through the forest until you come to a little pond" etc. They only tell you the 'coordinates' of the place (for example 1.27 mi S: GCG8V5), and you put them in your GPS and off you go! Oh, there's something else: The 'treasure' is usually several small things in a box (the so-called 'cache'!). You can take out as many as you want. But for every 'treasure' you take out, you have to put in something new.

The next day we started our geo-caching hunt. We looked for three hours, and we looked everywhere, behind every tree, under every stone, in every hole in the ground. Nothing! "Let's go back!" I said. Then suddenly Gillie shouted "Here it is!" She had her hand in a hole in the ground and when she took her hand out, I knew that it wasn't a cache! In her hand, my twelve-year-old

sister Gillie had a handful of old coins! Back at the camp, we showed the coins to Ron. He laughed. "Old coins? Ha, ha, ha! Good joke! They're not old. But give them to me!" Ron was very nice. He gave me a *Coldplay* CD and my sister a bar of chocolate for the coins! Later in the evening, Gillie showed me a coin. "I didn't give him this one," she said. "I wanted to keep it." 'Silly idea,' I thought. But I didn't say much. After all, she was only twelve.
Two days later there was a visit to a museum in a town near our camp. Ron went, so of course Gillie and I went along too. We saw lots of interesting things. Gillie suddenly shouted. "Look! The coins! The coins! They look like my coins!" Gillie was very excited. She looked at the coin in her hand. It looked exactly like the old Roman coins behind the glass window.

There was a man in uniform at the other end of the room. When Ron saw him, he got very nervous. "Be quiet, you silly girl!" he shouted. But the man in the uniform saw the coin. "Where did you find this coin?" he asked. "In the forest," Gillie said. "But not only this one. We found lots of them. And Ron's got them all. Ron's got them!"
Gillie pointed at Ron. Suddenly he did not look very cool any more. He turned around and ran away! Then things happened very quickly. The man in the uniform phoned the police. Two very friendly policemen came and took us to the police station in a car. "These coins are Roman coins. They're very old," one of them said. "And when you find old coins, you have to give them to the museum. Nobody can keep them! We're going to find this young man, Ron. He has to give the coins to the museum!"
Two days later the police found Ron. They took the coins away from him. They are now behind glass in the museum. And next to them is a little sign:

Roman coins (AD 42)
Found by Gillie Woodhouse

Gillie is very proud of this. Well, after all, she is only twelve …

8 Match the sentence halves.

1 Gillie and her brother Chris	[2] surprise activities.
2 They really liked the	[4] but they found some coins.
3 One day they took part in a geo-caching	[5] him the coins.
4 Chris and his sister didn't find the cache,	[1] went to an adventure holiday camp.
5 Ron laughed when the children showed	[7] very old.
6 Two days later the children went to a	[3] treasure hunt with Ron, one of the guides.
7 They found out that their coins were	[8] Ron and now they're in the museum.
8 The police took the coins away from	[6] museum in a town near their camp.

9 Look at the text again. Find the answers to these questions.

1 What do you have to have for geo-caching?
2 What do you have to do when you take something out from a cache?
3 What do you have to do when you find old coins?

WB p. 44

The Story of the Stones 3 The new girl

1 Match the sentence halves to complete the summary of Episode 2.

1 The children tell Sunborn
2 The children learn that
3 Sunborn tells the children
4 Sunborn gives the stones
5 The children morph

[2] Darkman is alive.
[4] to the children.
[1] about their dreams.
[5] into animals.
[3] the story of the stones.

2 Look at the picture from Episode 3 and say what you can see. What do you think happens in this episode?

3 Watch Episode 3 and put the sentences in order to tell the story.

[2] The children hear a cry for help.
[6] The children learn the new girl's name is Gillian.
[5] The tiger rescues the girl.
[1] The children talk about their dreams.
[4] Emma morphs and jumps in the river.
[3] Daniel thinks it's a trap.

Everyday English

4 Watch Episode 3 again. Match the pictures with the expressions.

I'm off now. Too late ... ! Poor you! Hang on.

Writing *for your Portfolio*

■ **10** **Sam is at a youth camp. Read her letter to her mum. Which paragraph (1, 2 or 3) talks about:**

a) what she did yesterday? .... **b)** the rules of the camp? ....
c) all the different things you can do at the camp? ....

Hi Mum,

c [1] The camp is really great! There are lots of things to do here like football and volleyball, for example.
We can go horse riding too.
We can go swimming in the river – it's fantastic!
We never get bored.

a [2] Yesterday I went on a great canoeing trip! We went down the river for two hours and then we had a picnic. Jack, our guide, made a fire and we sang songs and played games.

b [3] Everything is great, but of course there are rules. We have to go to bed at ten. We have to help in the kitchen. We have to make our beds. But we don't have to wash up – that's good.

I hope you and Dad are well. See you soon.
Love, Sam

SbX ■ **11** **Imagine you are at youth camp. Write a letter home to your parents.**

SbX

Grammar *have to / don't have to*

You **have to** wear a life jacket. You **don't have to** come along.

Write *have to* or *don't have to*.

Mit ¹.. sagst du, dass etwas **notwendig** ist.
Mit ².. sagst du, dass etwas **nicht notwendig** ist.

MORE fun with Fido!

UNIT 8 We might go out

Get talking Intentions

1 What are these people's plans? Talk about them with your partner. Use the words in the box to help you.

watch a DVD	do the shopping	tidy (your) room	play basketball
do (your) homework	stay at a friend's house	have a party	do nothing

A What's she going to do?

B She's going to do her homework.

6 CD 2 SbX

2 Listen to the dialogues and tick the correct box.

	Sharon	Nick	Chloe	Bill
have a party				
do nothing				
do homework				
stay at a friend's place				

7 CD 2

3 Read and complete the dialogues with the phrases in the box. There are two phrases you don't need. Listen and check.

No, I haven't	Do you want to come	What about you
I'd love to	She didn't invite me	And your school project

DIALOGUE 1

Steve Have you got any special plans for the weekend?

Luke [1] ....
I'm going to do nothing.

Steve What about TV?

Luke No, I'm not going to watch TV, there's nothing good on.

Steve [2] ....?

Luke No, I'm not going to do any homework. I'm going to do nothing!

DIALOGUE 2

Kevin What are your plans for the weekend?

Dawn Well, I'm going to watch DVDs tomorrow night. Do you want to watch them with me?

Kevin [3] .... , but I can't.

Dawn Oh, why not?

Kevin I'm going to Jenny's party.

Dawn [4] ....!

■ **4** **In pairs, practise the dialogues.**

SbX

Grammar *going to* (negative)

Du verwendest *going to*, wenn du etwas planst oder beabsichtigst, etwas zu tun.
Beim Zeitwort *go* verwendest du normaler Weise kein *going to*. Also: *I'm going to a party.*

So bildest du die Verneinung mit *going to*:
Negative of *be* + *going to* + *base form* of the verb.

I'm not going to play tennis tomorrow.
You **aren't going to** like the film.
He/she **isn't going to** do the shopping.
It **isn't going to** rain this afternoon.
We **aren't going to** do our homework.
They **aren't going to** play volleyball on Sunday.

Sounds right *going to*

8 CD 2 MP3 ● **5** **When we say *going to*, it often sounds like *gonna*. Listen and repeat.**

I'm going to write a letter,
I'm going to put it in the post.
And the letter's going to tell you
that I love you the most.

Get talking *Plans for the weekend*

● **6** **Find out about your partner's plans this weekend.**

A Are you going to watch TV?

B No, I'm not. I'm going to watch DVDs. What about you?

Time for a sketch

9 CD 2 MP3

7 **Listen and read.**

On Strike

SCENE 1
Friday evening

Simon Look at this!
Sally Our jobs for the weekend.
Simon It's too much!
Sally Yes. Let's go on strike!

SCENE 2
Later on Friday evening

Mum Hello – what's this?
Simon We're on strike.
Dad On strike?
Sally Yes – we're not going to tidy our rooms!
Simon And we're not going to do the shopping.
Sally I'm not going to do the washing-up.
Simon And I'm not going to put the rubbish out.
Dad OK.
Sally Excuse me?
Mum That's OK.
Simon Really? Great!

SCENE 3
Saturday morning

Sally Mum? Can I have bacon and eggs for breakfast, please?
Mum Yes – but I'm not going to make it.
Sally Pardon?
Mum I'm on strike!
Simon Dad? I'm going to be late for the football match.
Dad I know. But I'm not going to take you in the car.
Simon Excuse me?
Dad I'm on strike, too.
Mum We're on strike this weekend. We're not going to do things for you.
Dad That's right. We're only going to do things for …
Mum +Dad Us!!!
Sally Oh!
Simon Ah!

★ **8** **Practise the sketch in groups of four.**

WB pp. 48, 49 CYBER HOMEWORK 15

Story time

SbX

9 **Read the story.**

Grammar *might (not)*

Wenn du sagen willst, dass etwas möglicherweise (nicht) eintreten wird, verwendest du *might (not)* + *base form* of the verb.

I **might go** to the party. I'm not sure.
It **might rain**, so take a coat.
I **might not** sleep well.

He might not sleep well tonight.

■ **10 Here are some more of William's worries. Match the sentence halves.**

1 I don't want to go to the beach –
2 I don't want to go skiing –
3 I'm going to study tonight –
4 I don't want to go near that dog –
5 I don't want to answer the teacher's question –
6 I don't want to ride your bike –
7 I'm not going to eat that –
8 I'm not going to play 'trick or treat' –

☐ I might break my leg.
☐ I might not get it right.
☐ I might fall off.
☐ it might be poisonous.
☐ the sun might be too hot.
☐ I might get into trouble.
☐ we might have a test tomorrow.
☐ it might bite.

■ **11 Work in pairs. Take turns to test your partner.**

A Why doesn't William want to go to the beach?

B Because the sun might be too hot.

A That's right.

A Song 4 U *Weekend*

10/11 CD 2 MP3

12 Listen and sing.

It's the weekend! End of the week!
It's the weekend! End of the week!

No more lessons for a day or two.
It's the weekend. It's the weekend.
Stay in bed all day – got nothing to do.
It's the weekend. It's the weekend.

Get up late, then you phone a friend.
At the weekend. At the weekend.
The computer's on, I've got emails to send.
At the weekend. At the weekend.

It's the weekend …

Sunday night and it's over again.
End of the weekend. End of the weekend.
Goes too quickly. It's always the same.
End of the weekend. End of the weekend.
It's the weekend! End of the week!

It's the weekend …

CYBER HOMEWORK 16

Writing for your Portfolio

● 13 **Choose one of the texts below and answer the following questions:**

Why is there a party?
When and where is it?
What is there going to be there?

Text 1

Hi Kenny,
It's my birthday on Friday and I'm going to have a party on Saturday at my place. There's going to be lots of food and drink and there's going to be a DJ too. It's going to be great. The party starts at 6 p.m. Don't be late.
See you on Saturday,

Jill

Text 2

Hi Lisa,
There's going to be a fancy dress party at my school on Friday evening. Please come with me. I'm going as a pirate. Why don't you go as Catwoman like last year? There's going to be a DJ, and there's going to be lots and lots of food. At midnight there's going to be a special surprise! The party starts at six and finishes at half past twelve. Please say yes. My dad can take you home after the party. See you,

Fred

★ 14 **Now write a short email inviting a friend to your party. Think about your answers to the questions to help you.**

WB p. 51

UNIT 9 Strange things from space!

MP3 SbX

1 Look at the pictures. Put them in the right order. Write numbers.

The UFO

12 CD 2

2 Listen to the story and check.

Story time

13 CD 2 MP3

3 **Read the story. Then listen to it.**

The president of the planet Trojan spoke to all the people.

"People of Trojan!" she said. "I'm sorry, but I have bad news for you. Two months ago, we found out that a planet is coming towards us. A hundred years from now, the other planet is going to hit us, and the planet Trojan is going to explode. We can't stop this – it's going to happen."

The Trojan people were very scared. The president said more. "People of Trojan, we have only got one hundred years. But we've got a plan. We're going to build spaceships – huge spaceships, the biggest spaceships in the history of the universe. Each spaceship is going to be big enough to carry 10,000 people – and we are going to build 20,000 spaceships! In this way, we can take every Trojan man, woman and child to another place – a safe place – before the other planet hits us."

The people asked: "Where? Where is this place that we can all go to?"

The president said: "There is another planet, very far from here. It is a planet where Trojan people can live. The air is like our air; the water is like our water; and there is room for us. The name of this planet is: Earth! Earth is going to be our new home. Now, we have to get ready!"

The next day, the people of Trojan started to build the spaceships. It took them a very long time – more than fifteen years – to build the first 1,000 spaceships. And after fifty years, 5,000 spaceships were ready. And finally, all the 20,000 spaceships were ready. The spaceships were round, like huge yellow footballs – so big that 10,000 Trojans could go inside.

Then, one day, the people of Trojan said goodbye to their home. They went into the spaceships. And, one by one, the spaceships took off. And the Trojans began the journey to their new home.

Twenty years later, the spaceships arrived at the planet Earth.

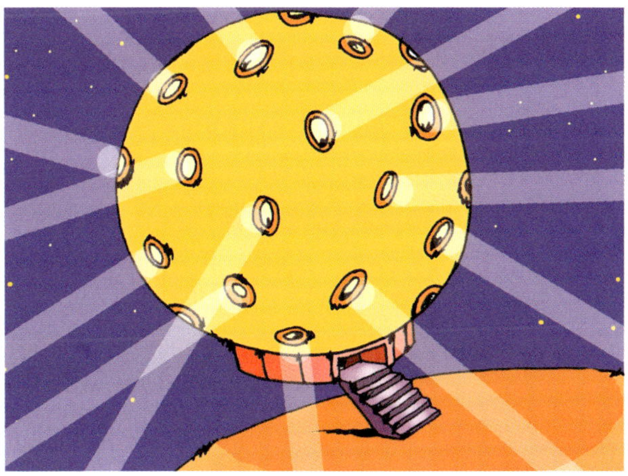

SbX

4 **Match the sentence halves.**

1	Another planet was going to	☐	into each spaceship.
2	The Trojan people planned	☐	20,000 very big spaceships.
3	The Trojan people built	☐	hit the planet Trojan.
4	10,000 Trojan people went	☐	at the planet Earth.
5	After twenty years, the Trojan people arrived	☐	to travel to Earth.

14 CD 2 MP3

5 Read Part 2 of the story. Then listen to it.

One day, Jenny was in her garden. It was a nice, sunny morning. Her dog, Josh, was with her – and suddenly he started to bark very loudly.

"What's the matter, Josh?" she said, and she walked over to him. In the air, there were lots of strange, round, yellow seeds. The seeds fell from the sky, and one by one they landed on the grass. Jenny looked around – there were thousands of the seeds on the ground. Just then, her father came out of the house.

"What are you looking at, Jenny?" he asked.

"Come here, Dad," she said. "Look at this!"

Her father came over and looked at the yellow seeds.

"How strange!" he said. "But I haven't got time to look at them now. I've got to go to work. Jenny, tidy up here, please!" And her father walked to his car. He walked on some of the seeds and they went 'crack!!' Jenny's father got into his car and went to work. Jenny went into the house.

She got a broom and came back to the garden. Then she started to sweep up the little yellow seeds. She put them into the dustbin.

6 Tick the correct answer.

1 Jenny's dog barked. He saw … a) strange seeds. b) a cat. c) Jenny's father.

2 Her father thought the seeds were … a) strange. b) beautiful. c) dirty.

3 He asked Jenny to … a) get into the car. b) go into the house. c) tidy the garden.

4 She put the seeds … a) in the house. b) in her father's car. c) into the dustbin.

7 What do you think the yellow seeds were?

Vocabulary Science fiction

SbX

8 Match the words and the drawings.

1 spaceship **2** galaxy **3** alien **4** time machine **5** astronaut **6** space station

Sounds right /ɪd/ /d/ /t/

15 CD 2

9 Which is the odd one out? Listen and check.

1 arrived landed planned **2** looked started barked **3** asked walked visited

WB p. 54 CYBER HOMEWORK 17

10 Complete the sentences. Use the verbs in the box in the *past simple*.

see pick go ~~be~~ hear put see turn

They never saw him again!

James ..was.. alone in a town.

He .... a strange noise.

He .... round.

He .... a gold key on the ground.

He .... it up.

He .... a green light in a window.

He .... the key in the door of the house.

He ....into the house.

11 Write the story.

Sentence 1: One day …
Sentence 2: Suddenly …
Sentences 3, 4 and 5: He …
Sentence 6: Then …
Sentence 7: At that moment …
Sentence 8: Finally, …

Writing *for your Portfolio*

12 Here are two endings for the story. Choose the one you like best and say why.

a) James went into the house. He saw a chair and he sat down. It was very comfortable! Then he found a button on the floor, near the chair. "What's this?" he said, and he pushed the button. The chair started to go round and round, very quickly, but after a minute, it stopped. James went out of the house. He was in the year 2090!

b) James went into the house. He saw a chair and he sat down. It was very comfortable! He went to sleep. Five hours later, James woke up. In front of him were two strange people with pink eyes. "Why are you here?" said one of the strange people. "You shouldn't be here! Now we have to take you to our planet!"

★ 13 Write another ending.

WB p. 55

The Story of the Stones 4 You can run, but you can't hide

1 **Answer the questions about Episode 3. Tick the right answers.**

1 Where were the children?	a) on the beach	b) by a river	c) by a lake
2 Who jumped in the water?	a) the eagle	b) the rat	c) the tiger
3 What is the new girl's name?	a) Lillian	b) Gillian	c) Debbie
4 Why was she in the water?	a) to save a cat	b) to save a dog	c) to save a rabbit

2 **Complete the summary of Episode 3 with *Gillian, Emma, Sarah* or *Darkman*.**

1 .... goes to Emma's house and gives the children a box of chocolates. Gillian tells them that she met a strange man. The children were worried it was probably 2 .... He wanted to know about the kids.
Before she leaves, Gillian gives them a box that 3 .... gave to her. 4 .... opens the box. A gas escapes. She and 5 .... are unconscious. 6 .... returns and saves them. 7 .... tells her about the morphing.

3 **Watch Episode 4 and match the questions with the answers.**

1 Why did Emma tell Gillian about the morphing?
2 Why does Sunborn want to give Gillian morphing powers?
3 Why does Gillian want them to close the door quickly?
4 Why doesn't Gillian want to join the team?
5 Why does Darkman break into the house?

☐ Because he wants the stones.
☐ Because she can help them make a stronger team.
☐ Because she doesn't like fighting.
☐ Because Darkman is after her.
☐ Because she saw the eagle on the floor.

Everyday English

4 **Watch Episode 4 again. Complete the sentences.**

In that case Calm down One thing at a time Look

Gillian He was behind me. I know it.

Emma 1 .... , Gillian. You're safe here with us.

Sarah 2 .... – we know who this man is. His name's Darkman and he's after us.

Sunborn Sometimes I feel that Darkman is very close indeed.

Daniel 3 .... , I think we should give Gillian morphing powers.

Sunborn 4 .... , Daniel. First I have to meet her.

Grammar

SbX

Past simple (revision)

Bei regelmäßigen Verben (*regular* verbs) bildest du das *past simple*, indem du -*ed* anhängst:

open – open**ed** laugh – laugh**ed**
look – look**ed**

Es gibt auch viele unregelmäßige Verben (*irregular verbs*). Beispiele sind:

be – **was/were** go – **went**
take – **took** run – **ran**
come – **came** see – **saw**

Die Verneinung bildest du mit *didn't + verb*:
They **didn't believe** her.
She **didn't take** another photograph.

Was/were verneinst du mit *wasn't/weren't*.

Mr Brown didn't look before he opened the door.

SbX

Past time markers

So kannst du ausdrücken, wann sich etwas in der Vergangenheit ereignet hat.

Two months ago, we found out that a planet is coming towards us.
One day, Jenny was in her garden.
Then she started to sweep up the seeds.
The next day, they started building the spaceships.
After fifty years, five thousand spaceships were ready.
Twenty years later, the spaceships arrived at the planet Earth.
Finally, all the spaceships were ready.

WB pp. 56, 57
CYBER HOMEWORK 18

UNIT 10 Are you ready to order?

Vocabulary Food

16 CD 2 SbX

1 Listen and write the numbers.

1 peppers
2 pears
3 pork
4 chocolate ice cream
5 chicken
6 plums
7 lamb
8 rice pudding
9 peaches
10 onions
11 tomatoes
12 cabbage
13 strawberries
14 turkey
15 cheesecake
16 pancakes
17 grapes
18 pumpkin pie
19 potatoes
20 beef

2 Write the food words in your exercise book. Create 4 lists.

fruit vegetables meat desserts

17 CD 2

3 Listen and write the names of the people below the shopping baskets.

Henry Ella Jacob Laura

1

Jacob

2

Laura

3

Henry

4

Ella

4 Write the words.

ham
cheese
sausages
olives
mushrooms

mushrooms .... onions .... sausages .... cheese .... ham ....

SbX

5 Read the dialogue and write the names under the pizzas.

Waiter	Are you ready to order?
Mr Hutton	Yes, I think we are.
Mrs Hutton	I'd like a medium pizza with ham, cheese and tomatoes.
Waiter	And to drink?
Mrs Hutton	Mineral water, please.
Mr Hutton	And for me, a medium pizza, too, with ham, mushrooms, tomatoes and green peppers. And a cola.
Ben	I'd like a medium pizza with ham, sausage, cheese, mushrooms and olives.
Mrs Hutton	Ben, you never eat olives at home.
Ben	Mum, please!
Mrs Hutton	OK.
Waiter	And to drink?
Ben	A cola, please.
Vicky	I'd like a medium pizza with mushrooms, tomatoes, green peppers and sausage. And a glass of orange juice.
Waiter	Anything else?
Mr Hutton	I haven't got a knife and fork.
Waiter	I'll bring them straightaway.

a

Ben ....

b
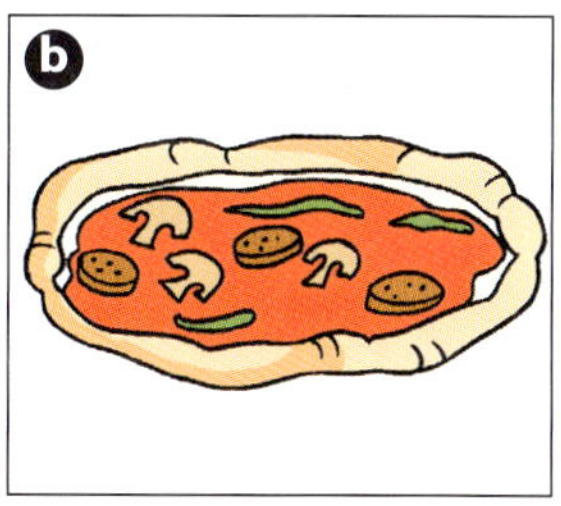
Vicky ....

c
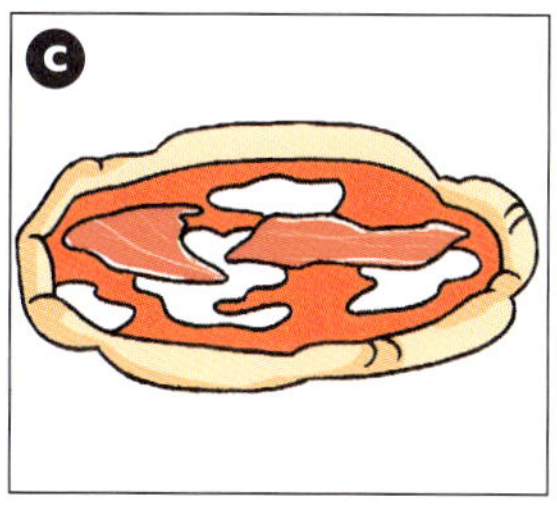
Mrs Hutton ....

d

Mr Hutton ....

18 CD 2 MP3

6 Listen to the dialogue and act it out.

WB p. 60 CYBER HOMEWORK 19

Time for a sketch

19 CD 2 MP3

7 **Listen and read.**

The best restaurant in town

SCENE 1

In the restaurant

Man A table for two, please.
Waiter Next to the window, sir?
Man That's fine.
Woman Can we have the menu please?
Waiter Certainly, madam. Straightaway. Can I get you something to drink?
Woman Mineral water, please.
Man The same for me.

2 minutes later

Waiter Here you are. Are you ready to order?
Woman Onion soup.
Man And the onion soup for me, too.
Waiter Thank you.

Menu

Starters:

Onion soup
Tomato soup

Main courses:

Lamb chops with potatoes and cabbage
Chicken with rice and peas
Beef with chips and carrots
Turkey with potatoes and cabbage
Pork chops with chips and peas

Desserts:

Chocolate ice cream
Cheesecake
Rice pudding
Pancakes
Pumpkin pie

SCENE 2

In the kitchen

Waiter Two onion soups and …
Chef Onion soup? We haven't got any onions.
Waitress I can run over to the supermarket and buy some.
Chef Too late. Let me think. Run over to Johnny's restaurant and get two bowls of onion soup.
Waitress OK.

5 minutes later

Chef But that's tomato soup.
Waitress They didn't have any onion soup.

SCENE 3

In the restaurant

Waiter I'm sorry. There isn't any onion soup. But we've got some tomato soup. It's a special recipe of the chef's grandma.
Woman OK. Bring us the tomato soup.

SCENE 4

In the restaurant

Waiter How did you like our chef's tomato soup?
Man It was fine. Now I'd like the beef with chips and carrots.
Woman And for me, the lamb with potatoes and cabbage.
Waiter Certainly.

SCENE 5

In the kitchen

Waiter One beef and one lamb.
Chef Is there any lamb in the fridge?
Waitress No, there isn't.
Chef What about beef? Have we got any beef?
Waitress No, sorry, there isn't any beef.
Chef What can we do?
Waitress Johnny's restaurant does a good chicken.
Chef Run over and get two chickens.

SCENE 6

In the restaurant

Waiter Here you are.
Woman But we ordered lamb and beef.
Waiter Madam, the chicken is the best in town. It's the chef's special recipe. Chicken Volcano.
Woman OK. The chicken then.

SCENE 7

In the kitchen

Waiter Run over to Johnny's again and get some rice pudding and chocolate ice cream.
Waitress OK.

SCENE 8

In the restaurant

Waiter For dessert we have rice pudding and chocolate ice cream.
Woman That's fine.
Waiter Here you are.
Man Look. There's a flag on my ice cream. It says: 'Johnny's restaurant'.
Woman I don't think we're in the best restaurant in town. Next time we're going to Johnny's.

8 Circle T *(True)* or F *(False)*.

1 The man and the woman want to have onion soup.	T / F
2 The chef sends the waitress to Johnny's restaurant to get some tomato soup.	T / F
3 There isn't any lamb in the fridge, but there is some beef.	T / F
4 The man and the woman have chicken.	T / F
5 The rice pudding and the ice cream are not from Johnny's restaurant.	T / F
6 The man finds a flag on his ice cream.	T / F

WB pp. **61, 62**

A Song 4 U *A slice of pizza*

20/21 CD 2 MP3

9 Listen and sing.

Have you got a pizza
with pepper, ham and cheese?
Have you got a pizza?
Then give it to me, please.

Oh, please be so nice.
Give me, oh give me a slice,
with lots of cheese.
We want some pizza, please.

Yummy, yummy!
Pizza, ice cream for my tummy.
Yummy, yummy!
Pizza, ice cream for my tummy.

Can I have some ice cream –
chocolate, lemon, peach?
Can I have some ice cream?
I'd like a bit of each.

Oh, please be so sweet.
Give me, o give me a treat.
Two scoops or three
of sweet strawberry.

Yummy, yummy! …

Writing *for your Portfolio*

10 Read the text.

Last Sunday my dad and I went to a restaurant. We had tomato soup and a pizza. Suddenly dad stopped eating. There was something under the cheese. It was the top of a salt cellar. Dad called the waiter. The waiter said sorry and dad got another pizza.

To make a text more interesting, add some dialogue and some details:

Last Sunday my dad and I went to a restaurant. We had tomato soup and then Dad had a pizza with extra cheese and I had spaghetti. Suddenly Dad stopped eating. "What's the matter?" I asked. "I don't know," Dad said. "There's something under the cheese." "Yeah," I said, "your pizza." "Very funny," Dad said. Then he lifted the cheese.

★ **11 Choose one of the pictures. Write a story about it.**

SbX

Grammar *some* and *any*

Run over to the supermarket and buy **some** tomatoes. (= einige Tomaten)
Du verwendest in diesem Satz *some*, weil nicht angegeben wird, wie viele Tomaten es sind.

Get **some** rice pudding and chocolate ice cream. (= etwas Reispudding)
In diesem Satz sagst du *some*, weil du von etwas sprichst, das man nicht zählen kann.

We haven't got **any** onions. (= keine Zwiebel)
Hier verwendest du *any*, weil du ausdrücken willst, dass etwas *nicht vorhanden* ist.

There isn't **any** onion soup. But we've got **some** tomato soup.
Hier sagst du, dass etwas *nicht vorhanden* ist (die Zwiebelsuppe), aber etwas anderes *vorhanden* ist (die Tomatensuppe).

Read the questions and answers. Write *some* and *any*.

Have we got **any** beef?
Can I have **some** ice cream?
Mit 1 ...some... fragst du nach etwas, von dem du weißt, dass es vorhanden ist.
Mit 2 ...any... fragst du, ob etwas vorhanden ist.

22 CD 2

12 Fill in *some* or *any*. Then listen and check.

Dad Sue, are there 1 .... plums and peaches?
Sue There are 2 .... plums, but there aren't 3 .... peaches. Are you making fruit salad?
Dad Yes. What have we got?
Sue There are 4 .... grapes and 5 .... pears.
Dad OK. Are there 6 .... strawberries?
Sue No, sorry Dad. There aren't 7 ....

WB p. 63 CYBER HOMEWORK 20

Kids in NYC 2

The baseball star

Before you watch

1 Write the words under the pictures.

team
pitch
bat
hit

1.................. 2.................. 3.................. 4..................

2 In what order do you think the pictures come in the DVD? Write 1-4.

A ☐

B ☐

C ☐

D ☐

Watch the story

3 Check your answers to 2.

4 Circle the correct answer.

1 Emma *likes* / *doesn't like* baseball.
2 Gerry is *tall* / *short* with blue eyes.
3 The boys have got a big game on *Thursday* / *Friday*.
4 Emma wants to *pitch* / *hit* a few balls.

5 Circle T *(True)* or F *(False)*.

1	Emma is a new student at East Central High.	T / F
2	Gerry Wood has blonde hair and blue eyes.	T / F
3	Steve doesn't want Emma to play baseball.	T / F
4	Emma plays baseball on the school team.	T / F
5	The ball hits Gerry on the arm.	T / F

6 Complete the dialogue.

reddish
new
interesting
tall
great
fair

Emma I love watching baseball.
Jenny You love watching baseball or you love watching Gerry Wood play baseball?
Emma Which one's Gerry Wood? Remember, I'm [1] .... at the school.
Jenny He's pitching now. He's [2] .... with [3] .... hair and blue eyes.
Emma He seems [4] .... But I'm more interested in the baseball.
Jenny Really?
Emma Yeah, what a [5] .... game. Why can't girls play? It isn't [6] ....
Jenny Do girls want to play baseball?
Emma Well, I do.

Everyday English

7 Complete the dialogues.

By the way,
It's no trouble at all.
It isn't fair.

Progress Check Units 6–10

Listening

23 CD 2

Listen. Where are they? Write the first letters on the maps.

B = bank **C** = cinema **CH** = chemist's **SC** = shopping centre

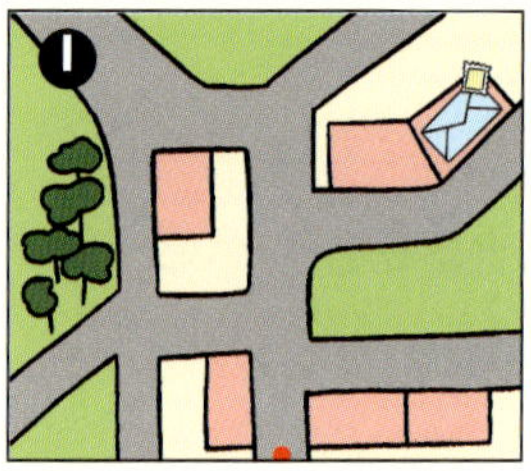

☐ 4

Reading

Read the story. For each paragraph, choose a title from the box. Write the numbers. Careful – there are six titles, but there are only five paragraphs.

1 Jenny falls asleep
2 Jenny's father finds something
3 Jenny reads a great story
4 The pictures in Jenny's head
5 1,000 years in space
6 A face from space

A big surprise for Jenny

○ In the afternoon Jenny was in the house. She had her favourite book in her hands, Life on planet XRJ. It was a great story about 2 young people, Joanna and Ken. They had a spaceship and visited strange planets in it. They had lots of exciting adventures together.

○ Jenny liked the story a lot. In her head, she saw pictures of Joanna and Ken in their spaceship, and she saw beautiful pictures of the Earth, of strange planets in space, and people living there.

○ It was warm and quiet in the room. Jenny was very, very tired, and so she closed her eyes for a few minutes. She slept for 2 or 3 hours.

○ Then her father came into the house. "Look what I've found in the garden," said her father. "These seeds are not from trees. They're strange, really strange." He put the yellow seed on Jenny's hand and then left the room.

○ Suddenly Jenny heard a strange noise. It came from the seed. Then the seed became red, blue and yellow. "Is this a dream?" Jenny thought. "No, it's not! We're real!" Somebody spoke. She looked at the seed. There was a door in it. It was open, and Jenny could see the face of a little green man ...

☐ 5

Grammar

Circle the correct answer.

1 It's really cold today. You *have to / don't have to* wear an anorak.
2 There's no English test on Monday. I *have to / don't have to* study at the weekend.
3 Don't read this book. You *aren't going to / didn't* like it.
4 Dave is ill. *He's not going to play / He does not play* for the school team tomorrow.
5 Look at the black clouds. It *can / might* rain soon.
6 **A** Are you going to Jean's party?
  B I'm not sure. I *can / might.*
7 Two months ago, Sue's parents *was / were* in London.
8 Tony wasn't hungry, so he *ate / didn't eat* the pizza.
9 Sorry, there isn't *some / any* ice cream.
10 I'm hungry. Are there *some / any* restaurants here?

☐ 10

Vocabulary

Write the words under the pictures.

❶  ❷  ❸  ❹ 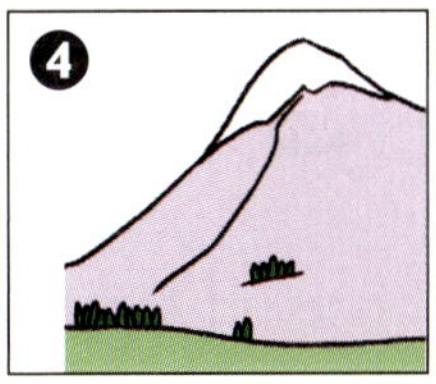 ❺ 

....

☐ 5

Dialogue

Complete the dialogue. There are three phrases you do not need.

for the weekend	going to be back	tidy my room	I'm going to
lucky you	do you want to come	nothing special	let's visit them

Judy Hey, Nick. What are your plans [1] .... ?
Nick [2] .... What about you?
Judy Let's go canoeing on Saturday.
Nick Canoeing? Sounds interesting. But [3] .... Ken's party on Saturday.
Judy No, problem, we're [4] .... at 4 o'clock. [5] ....?
Nick I'm not sure, but it sounds great. I think I might.

☐ 5

How did you do?

Listening	☺ 4	😐 2-3	☹ 0-1
Reading	☺ 4-5	😐 2-3	☹ 0-1
Grammar	☺ 7-10	😐 4-6	☹ 0-3
Vocabulary	☺ 4-5	😐 2-3	☹ 1
Dialogue	☺ 4-5	😐 2-3	☹ 0-1
Total	☺ 19-29	😐 6-18	☹ 0-5

UNIT 11 The curse of the pharaoh

Vocabulary Ancient Egypt

24 CD 2 SbX

1 Listen and write the numbers. Where in the picture can you see the following things?

- a papyrus
- a pyramid
- a mummy
- a tomb
- a sphinx
- a temple
- hieroglyphics

25 CD 2

2 Are you good at history? Do the quiz about ancient Egypt and find out. (There is more than one right answer to question number 6.) Then listen and check.

– ANCIENT EGYPT QUIZ –

1 What was the name of the Egyptian kings?
a) presidents ☐ b) lords ☐ c) pharaohs ☐ d) emperors ☐

2 What was the most sacred animal of the Egyptians?
a) the cow ☐ b) the goose ☐ c) the crocodile ☐ d) the cat ☐

3 A Sphinx has a human head and the body of …
a) a snake ☐ b) a lion ☐ c) a hippo ☐ d) an elephant ☐

4 A river was very important for the ancient Egyptians. What is its name?
a) the Amazon ☐ b) the Thames ☐ c) the Nile ☐ d) the Seine ☐

5 Religion was very important for the Egyptians. This is why they built lots of …
a) cathedrals ☐ b) altars ☐ c) crosses ☐ d) pyramids and temples ☐

6 Which of these did the ancient Egyptians invent?
a) bathrooms ☐ b) eye glasses ☐ c) knives ☐ d) paper ☐

26 CD 2 MP3

3 Read the text. Then listen to it.

LIFE IN ANCIENT EGYPT

Q How do we know what life in ancient Egypt was like?

A From documents written on papyrus, from hieroglyphics on stones, and from wall paintings and objects found in tombs.

Q What did people wear?

A People only wore light clothes because it was very hot. They wore sandals on their feet or they went barefoot. The sandals were made of palm leaves. Slaves, workers and children were often naked. People cared a lot about their looks. Men and women wore eye make-up and jewellery. They also used perfumes.

Q What work did the Egyptians do?

A Many Egyptians worked as farmers. They worked on the fields, but they also helped to build the pyramids and temples. There were also other jobs. Weavers, for example, made beautiful clothes. They sold the clothes to other people. People paid for the clothes with food, salt and other things.

Q What did people eat?

A The Egyptians had lots of different food. They hunted fish, ducks and geese. Many people were farmers and had sheep, cattle, goats, pigs, and later also horses. These animals gave them milk, wool, meat and eggs. But they also used the leather, the horns and the fat. The Egyptians even had farms where they kept oxen. They also had lots of vegetables and fruit.

Q What did people do in their free time?

A Hunting and fishing were the most popular sports for the men. Children played with balls and animals made from wood. Rich Egyptians often gave big parties with lots of food and drink. There were musicians, singers, dancers, jugglers and acrobats. Servants put big pieces of perfumed fat on people's heads. When the fat melted, it ran down their faces. This made them smell nice.

4 Circle T *(True)* or F *(False)*.

1	Some people in Egypt did not wear clothes.	T / F
2	Men wore make-up and used perfumes too.	T / F
3	Only slaves built the pyramids.	T / F
4	Weavers got a lot of money for their work.	T / F
5	The Egyptians ate meat, vegetables and fruit.	T / F
6	Children went hunting and fishing.	T / F

★ 5 Go through 2 and 3 and underline the plural forms of the following words:

man   child   woman   person   foot   goose   fish   knife   leaf   ox

WB p. 67   CYBER HOMEWORK 21

SbX

6 Read about the pyramids at Giza. Put the numbers where you think they go.

100,000 230 20 143 2 million 2,000

The pyramids in Egypt are the tombs of the pharaohs. The biggest pyramid is the one for the Pharaoh Khufu. Did you know?

1 It is [1] .... metres high, and each side is more than [2] .... metres long.
2 There are more than [3] .... stone blocks in the pyramid.
3 Each stone is about [4] .... kilograms.
4 More than [5] .... men worked to build it.
5 It took more than [6] .... years to build it.

27 CD 2

7 Listen to the interview and check your answers.

8 Read more about the pyramids and answer the questions below.

When a pharaoh died, the priests put the mummy inside a pyramid. The Egyptian people believed that after a long time, the pharaoh's spirit woke up. Then it climbed up the steps of the pyramid to meet Ra, the sun god. They also believed that when the pharaoh woke up, he needed many things – for example, food, clothes and jewellery. The people put these things in the pyramid with the mummy.
Of course, everyone knew there were wonderful things inside the pyramid.

Soldiers guarded the tombs day and night to stop thieves. But hundreds of years later, robbers found many of the tombs and stole everything inside.
One of the most famous pharaohs was Tutankhamun. He became pharaoh when he was nine, but he died when he was only nineteen. He is famous because the robbers did not find his tomb. When an Englishman called Howard Carter found the tomb of Tutankhamun in 1922, it was still full of wonderful clothes and jewellery.

1 Who put the mummy in the pyramids? ....
2 Who met the pharaoh's spirit at the top of the pyramid? ....
3 Who was Ra? ....
4 Who guarded the tombs? ....
5 Who died when he was only 19? ....
6 Who found Tutankhamun's tomb? ....

Sounds right /dʒ/ /tʃ/

28 CD 2 MP3

9 Listen and repeat the tongue-twister. How quickly can you say it?

Jim juggles jam
and Chuck chooses chickens.

Story time

29 CD 2 MP3

10 **Read the text. Then listen to it.**

THE STORY OF HOWARD CARTER

Howard Carter was born in England in 1874. He was very interested in history. When he was 17, he went to Egypt. He had one wish – he wanted to find the tomb of Tutankhamun. Another Englishman, Lord Carnarvon, had the same dream. He gave Howard some money to find the tomb. For five years Carter tried to find it, but he didn't find anything.

Then he went back to England. When he returned to Egypt, he brought a yellow canary with him. "A golden bird!" shouted one of the Egyptian workers. "The bird will show us the tomb!"

On November 4th, 1922, Carter's workmen discovered the tomb of a pharaoh. Carter wanted to open it the next day. When he came back to his house that night, his servant came up to him and said: "A snake killed your yellow bird. I'm sure it was the pharaoh's snake. Don't open the tomb! There is a curse on the tomb – the curse of the pharaoh! It can kill hundreds of people and animals." But Carter didn't listen to him.

He sent a telegram to Lord Carnarvon in England. Carnarvon arrived in Egypt on November 26th. Carter made a hole in the door of the tomb. He took a candle and looked inside. Behind him, Lord Carnarvon asked: "Can you see anything?" Carter answered: "Yes, wonderful things!" In the tomb there were lots of treasures. There was also the mummy of the boy-king, Pharaoh Tutankhamun!

A few days later an insect bit Lord Carnarvon on the left cheek. He became ill and died. Back in England, his dog died on the same day.

When workmen took off the bandages from the mummy of Tutankhamun, they saw that there was also a wound on the pharaoh's left cheek.

Was there really a curse of the pharaoh?

11 **Put the sentences in the correct order. Write numbers.**

- [ ] But Howard Carter didn't listen. He sent a telegram to Lord Carnarvon.
- [1] When Howard Carter was seventeen, he went to Egypt.
- [ ] His servant was scared and said, "Don't open it! There's a curse!"
- [ ] One day, his workmen discovered a tomb.
- [ ] He wanted to find the tomb of Tutankhamun.
- [ ] They found lots of treasures inside, and the mummy of Tutankhamun.
- [ ] When Lord Carnarvon arrived, they opened the tomb.

WB p. 68

Story time

30 CD 2 MP3 SbX ★

(12) **Read the story. Then listen to it.**

THE CURSE OF THE PHARAOH

First Hannah, Luke and their parents looked at the pictures on the walls in the tourist centre. They showed scenes from ancient Egypt. There were hundreds of farmers and slaves building a pyramid. Then they took a tour to one of the pyramids. Inside the pyramid it was so much cooler than in the hot sun.

"Stay with me all the time!" the guide said. "It's dangerous in here. There's a curse of the pharaoh!"

"The curse of the pharaoh?" asked another tourist in the group. "What's that?"

"There's one more tomb in this pyramid. But nobody knows where it is," said the guide. "A few years ago some scientists wanted to find it. They went into the pyramid, but they never came back. People say the curse of the pharaoh killed them!"

"The curse of the pharaoh!" Hannah laughed out loud. "But I'd love to find that tomb!" she whispered to Luke.

Luke didn't say anything. He had discovered a hole in the wall. "That's funny. The guide didn't say anything about this hole!" he said. "Let's go through here! I've got a torch so we can find our way back."

"Shh!!" said Hannah. "Mum and dad mustn't see us!" The two children climbed through the hole. Suddenly there was a loud noise and a second later a big stone filled the hole! Hannah and Luke tried to move the big stone. But they couldn't get out. "The curse of the pharaoh!" whispered Luke.

★ (12) **Match the sentence halves.**

1 Hannah, Luke and their parents
2 The guide told them
3 One of the stories
4 They tried to find a tomb in the pyramid,
5 The guide said
6 The children climbed
7 Suddenly there was
8 The children

☐ but never came back.
☐ through a hole in the wall.
☐ lots of stories about the pyramid.
☐ a loud noise and the hole was closed.
☐ went inside a pyramid with a guide.
☐ could not get out again.
☐ "The curse of the pharaoh killed them!"
☐ was about a group of scientists.

Get talking Completing a story

31 CD 2 ★

(14) **Say what you think happened next. Then listen and find out.**

WB p. 69

MORE! INFORMATION

Liebe Schülerin, lieber Schüler,

Wir sind überzeugt davon, dass du den Englischunterricht mit MORE! cool findest. Wichtig ist aber auch, dass du bei allem Spaß am Englischlernen nicht aufs Üben vergisst, damit du in der Fremdsprache mit Sicherheit immer fit bist!

Wer Englisch zu Hause intensiv üben möchte, kann dies am besten mit der **MORE! DVD-ROM (Lernsoftware)** tun. Sie bietet dir neben einem zielgerichteten Schularbeitentraining jede Menge abwechslungsreiche Übungen und unterhaltsame Spiele.

Auf der **MORE! Homepage** findest du zusätzlich ein kostenloses Angebot mit Downloads, interaktiven Lernspielen und Online Progress Checks.

Schau doch mal (am besten mit deinen Eltern) rein!

Viel Spaß beim Lernen – mit MORE!
wünscht dir das MORE!-Team

→ www.more-online.at

- Gratis MP3-Downloads aller Stories, Songs, Chants und Poems. So kannst du sie dir zu Hause nochmals in Ruhe anhören!
- Interaktive Lernspiele
- Online Progress Checks

MORE!

MORE! INFORMATION

Die MORE! ② DVD-ROM

Englischlernen am Computer macht nicht nur Spaß!
Mit der MORE! DVD-ROM* kann der Lernstoff zu Hause effizient gefestigt werden. Das Zusatz-Tool „Test-Training-Software" bietet dir außerdem die ideale Vorbereitung auf Tests und Schularbeiten.

Die MORE! DVD-ROM bietet:

- Animated cartoon stories
- Vocabulary games
- Dialogue karaoke
- Test-Training-Software – so trainierst du zu Hause für deine Schularbeiten
- Karaoke – so kann die ganze Familie Spaß mit den Liedern haben
- zahlreiche wertvolle Grammatikübungen
- intensives Wortschatztraining
- interaktive Ausspracheübungen
- tolle Hörverstehensübungen
- interessante Lesetexte
- Dialogübungen
- Kurzvideos zu den Time for Action-Stories im Buch
- Training zum Schreiben von Texten
- Diktate und
- Das MORE! Trivia Quiz!

* **Systemvoraussetzungen:**
Windows ME/2000/XP/VISTA/7, Pentium/Celeron/Athlon/Thunderbird 800+ MHz, Windows ME (128MB)/ 2000 & XP (256 MB)/VISTA/7 (512 MB), 16x DVD-ROM Laufwerk, Soundkarte, Grafikkarte (High colour), mind. 300 MB Festplattenspeicherplatz, max. 2000 MB

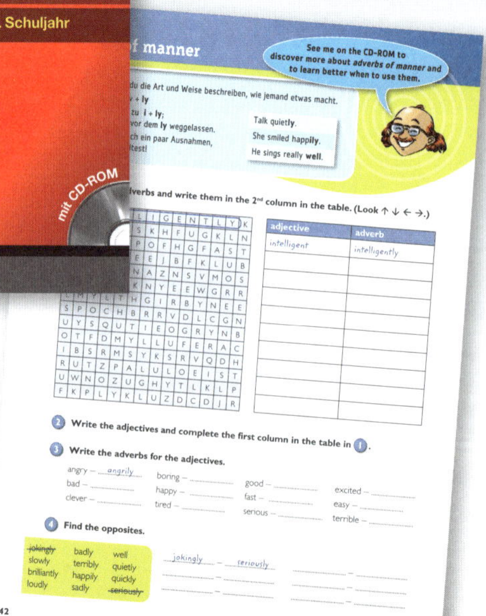

MORE! ② Grammar Practice

Dieses Übungsheft mit CD-ROM bietet auf 64 Seiten zusätzliche Übungen zu allen wesentlichen Grammatikinhalten von MORE! 2. An den Themen und damit an der Wortschatzprogression von MORE! orientiert, kannst du dich speziell auf die grammatikalischen Aufgabenstellungen konzentrieren, ohne vorher neue Inhalte erarbeiten zu müssen.

Die dem Buch beiliegende CD-ROM bietet zusätzliche Übungen mit innovativen Features. Diese helfen dir komplexe grammatikalische Strukturen, deren alltägliche Verwendung und vor allem den Unterschied zur Grammatik der Muttersprache besser zu verstehen.

MORE! INFORMATION

Wer viel liest, kann bald besser Englisch!

Hast du Lust darauf, englischen Lesestoff zu Hause zu genießen? Die HELBLING READERS bieten dir Gelegenheit dazu!

HELBLING READERS – RED SERIES

The Surprise by Günter Gerngross
Als Tante Elizabeth aus Grönland zurückkommt, hat sie für Roger und Helen ein seltsames Geschenk im Gepäck – ein großes Ei. Eines Tages beginnt sich das Ei zu öffnen ...

Holly the Eco Warrior by Martyn Hobbs
Hollys Lieblingsplatz ist das Baumhaus in der alten Eiche im Garten. Als ihr Vater beschließt, den Baum zu fällen um ein Büro zu bauen, greift sie zu einer ungewöhnlichen Maßnahme und zieht in das Baumhaus. Wer wird den Kampf um den Baum gewinnen?

The African Mask by Günter Gerngross
Janet bekommt völlig überraschend einen Brief von ihrem alten Freund Donald McKinnon. Er lädt sie zu sich nach Schottland ein. Dort angekommen passieren seltsame Dinge. Warum ergreifen die Menschen die Flucht, sobald sie Donalds Namen hören? Warum ist Donald so traurig und was hat seine afrikanische Maske mit all den seltsamen Vorgängen zu tun?

Infos und Prospekte bei

HELBLING
Kaplanstraße 9
Postfach 12
A-6063 Rum
Tel. 0512 / 26 23 33-0
Fax 0512 / 26 23 33-111

E-Mail:
office@helbling.co.at

www.helblinglanguages.at

BESTELLKARTE für SchülerInnen!

Stück	Titel	Preis
	MORE!②-DVD-ROM mit Schularbeitentraining ISBN 978-3-85272-046-3	€ 39,90
	MORE!② Grammar Practice mit CD-ROM ISBN 978-3-85272-224-5	€ 14,90
	Holly the Eco Warrior, Martyn Hobbs Buch mit CD, 64 Seiten ISBN 978-3-902504-41-8	€ 8,90
	The African Mask, Günter Gerngross Buch mit CD, 32 Seiten ISBN 978-3-85272-028-9	€ 7,90
	The Surprise, Günter Gerngross Buch mit CD, 32 Seiten ISBN 978-3-85272-004-3	€ 7,90

Datum

Unterschrift (Bei Minderjährigen der Erziehungsberechtigte)

MORE! INFORMATION

Liebe Schülerin, lieber Schüler, liebe Eltern!

Auch fürs Englischlernen gilt: Übung macht den Meister/die Meisterin! Wer zu Hause regelmäßig übt, erzielt mit Sicherheit die besseren Leistungen.

MORE! bietet für das Üben zu Hause attraktive Materialien: die MORE! DVD-ROM, die MORE! Grammar Practice, die interessanten Lesehefte und die Tipps und Tricks im Internet.

Wie kann man die DVD-ROM, das Grammatikheft oder die Readers bestellen? Ganz einfach – Bestellkarte ausfüllen und an Helbling Languages schicken. Man kann die ausgefüllte Bestellkarte auch in einer Buchhandlung abgeben, um die gewünschten Produkte dort zu kaufen.

Viel Spaß beim Lernen – mit MORE!
wünscht dir das MORE!-Team

Einfach zu bestellen!

Die beiliegende Bestellkarte zum Ausschneiden einfach in einer Buchhandlung abgeben oder an folgende Adresse senden:

HELBLING Verlagsgesellschaft m.b.H. · Kaplanstraße 9 · Postfach 12 · 6063 Rum
Tel. 0512 / 26 23 33 - 0 · Fax 0512 / 26 23 33 - 111

Sie können auch via Internet bestellen.
Unsere E-Mail Adresse lautet: office@helbling.co.at

Oder besuchen Sie unsere Homepage. Hier finden Sie, neben unserem Bestellservice auch umfangreiche Poduktinformationen: www.helblinglanguages.at

Absender:
(Bitte in Blockschrift)

Vorname Familienname

Straße

Postleitzahl Ort

Schule (Name und Ort)

Bitte freimachen!

HELBLING LANGUAGES
Vertrieb f. Österreich
Helbling
Verlagsgesellschaft m.b.H.

Kaplanstraße 9
6063 Rum/Innsbruck

Writing *for your Portfolio*

★ **15** **Write an ending to Luke and Hannah's story. Use some of these words.**

farmers jewellery strange clothes food hot tired invite understand gold sleep thirsty happy ending hungry pharaoh

Start like this:
At first, Luke and Hannah did not know what to do.
They started to walk over to the people. Then …

SbX

Grammar Irregular plurals

Complete. Write *people/children/leaves/women/feet/teeth.*

Einige Nomen *(nouns)* sind unregelmäßig. Sie bekommen im *plural* kein s.

man	**men**	woman	1 …………………		
child	2 …………………	person	3 …………………		
foot	4 …………………	tooth	5 …………………	goose	**geese**

Einige Nomen *(nouns)* haben im *singular* und im *plural* die gleiche Form:
one fish – two **fish** one sheep – two **sheep**

Nomen, die auf *-f* oder *-fe* enden, bekommen im *plural* meist ein *ves*.
knife **knives** thief **thieves** leaf 6 …………………

SbX

Questions with "Who …?"

Wenn du mit *Who* …? nach dem Subjekt fragst, verwendest du kein *do/does* or *did*:
Who put the mummy in the pyramids? (**Not:** Who ~~did~~ put … ?)
Who found Tutankhamun's tomb? (**Not:** Who ~~did~~ find …?)

MORE fun with Fido!

UNIT 12 Families

Vocabulary Family

32 CD 2 SbX

1 Listen and write the first names.

William
Natasha
Anthony
Susan
Fred
Jo
Lisa

Get talking Who's who?

2 Work in pairs. Write down the first names of people in your family (uncles, cousins, grandparents etc.). Give the list to your partner. Your partner asks you who is who.

A Who's Susanne?
B She's my aunt.

A Who are Cindy and Jane?
B They're my cousins.

3 Read the text and match the sentence halves.

http://www.records.com/families

The world's largest family

Mr and Mrs Albina don't know where all their children are living now. They don't even know how old all their children are. And, of course, they don't know how many grandchildren or great-grandchildren they have.
The Albinas have 53 sons and daughters, and they are certainly the world's largest family. When people hear about the Albinas' large family, the first question they ask is: "How is it possible? How can one woman give birth to 53 children in her lifetime?" The answer is simple: Every time Mrs Albina gave birth, she had twins (two children) or triplets (three children).
They got married when Mrs Albina was 12 and Mr Albina was 30. Now Mr Albina is 77 years old, and Mrs Albina is 59. They live in a small town in Chile, and 18 of their children still live with them.

1 The Albinas don't know
2 The Albinas have
3 The Albinas got married
4 The Albinas live in a small
5 Eighteen children still live

☐ 47 years ago.
☐ with their mother and father.
☐ where all their children are living now.
☐ 53 children, all of them twins or triplets.
☐ town in Chile.

WB p. 74

SbX

4 **Read the text. Who likes doing what? Write the names under the activities.**

The Boehmer Family

The Boehmer family are a large family. There are the parents, Larry and Judy, and there are eleven children – seven girls and four boys. All of the Boehmer family are jugglers – and even the dog Bosco is part of the show. The first family show was in 1989 by Larry and three children, and by 1992 they were all in the show. Today they are the largest family of jugglers in the world. Every week they practise for 8 -10 hours for their shows. Of course, they are also interested in other things. Adam, the eldest son, likes working out, and Casey, the eldest daughter, likes water skiing and running. Sarah and Melissa like roller-skating. Margaret the youngest, likes playing with her "horsies" – and Rebecca likes learning new juggling tricks.

They all love doing the shows. "It's not very difficult", Larry says. "Anybody can do it. You must practise and practise, and you mustn't get lazy. But juggling doesn't need special talent."

....

Vocabulary Activities

33 CD 2 SbX

5 **Listen to what some of the other Boehmer children like doing. Tick the activities you hear.**

☐ climbing a tree
☐ dancing
☐ swimming
☐ playing basketball
☐ reading
☐ talking to my friends on the phone
☐ playing tennis
☐ going shopping

Get talking Favourite activities

6 **Work in pairs. Tell your partner what you like doing. Look at 4 and 5 for words.**

SbX **7** **Read the texts about the families and circle T *(True)* or F *(False)*.**

What's in a family?

I'm **Lisa,** and I'm from Galway in Ireland. My mum, my mum's friend Mike, my sister Hannah and I live in a large flat. Mike moved in with us three years ago. My real dad also lives in Galway, but he and mum aren't married anymore. He moved out five years ago, and now he lives in a little house with his new wife, Dorothy. Hannah and I go to see them every weekend. Mum says we are a single parent family, but I don't think so. We still see our father, and there are Mike and Dorothy. They're both very nice, and we have a lot of fun with them.

I'm **Amar** and I'm from Birmingham in England. I live with my mum and dad and my brother Vikas and my sister Karisma in a nice house in Selly Oak. My grandmother Jaya also lives with us, and for two years my cousin Kunal also lived in our house. He was here from Allahabad in India. He studied at the university in Birmingham. I like him, and next summer I'm going to visit him in Allahabad.

I'm **Les**. I'm from Sydney in Australia. My mum's a single parent and I live with her. My dad lives in Darwin and I don't often see him. I haven't got any brothers or sisters. My mum works in a restaurant, and I often stay with my grandparents. They live down the road. Sometimes I go and see my mum at the restaurant.

I'm **Denise**, and I'm from Angola, but I live in the Dukwi refugee camp in Botswana. We had to leave Angola eight years ago because of the war. Now my mum, my dad, my three brothers and my uncle João live in Dukwi camp. I go to school here. My brothers have to help my dad with farming. It's very hard work and we don't have much food.
My uncle João works for the Red Cross and translates from Portuguese into English. He likes his job.

1	Lisa sees her father every weekend.	T / F
2	Mike moved in with them five years ago.	T / F
3	Amar has two cousins and a sister.	T / F
4	Amar is going to Allahabad next weekend.	T / F
5	Les comes from a single parent family.	T / F
6	He always sleeps at his grandparents' place.	T / F
7	Denise and her family had to flee from Angola.	T / F
8	All her family work in the fields.	T / F

WB p. 75 CYBER HOMEWORK 23

■ **8** **Put the dialogue into the correct order. Then check with a partner. Act it out.**

☐ **Dad** Alright, but before you go you must help me with the dishes.
[1] **Dad** You must be home by 8. You mustn't be late!
☐ **Dad** I don't care about the others.
☐ **Rory** But Dad. That's not fair. All the others stay till ten.
☐ **Rory** But Dad, I just want to stay till ten.

34 CD2 ■ **9** **Listen to the dialogue between Fred and his mum. Tick the things he mustn't do.**

go into private files | delete a file | print out everything | chat | surf around

Sounds right *mustn't*

35 CD 2 MP3 ● **10** **Listen and repeat.**

I mustn't go here and I mustn't go there!
Well, you mustn't forget that life isn't fair. Woof!

Get talking Rules at home

■ **11** **Work in pairs. Tell your partner six things you must (*mustn't*) do at home.**

★ **12** **Read the anecdote. Guess which ending is the true one.**

The forgetful genius

The famous mathematician David Hilbert (1862–1943) was a genius, but he was also very absent-minded[1]. One day the Hilberts moved to another house. His wife gave him a little piece of paper and said. "David, we're moving today. I wrote the new address on this piece of paper." "Thank you," said Hilbert and put the piece of paper into his jacket. At the university, he needed a piece of paper to make some notes. He took the paper out of his jacket. He wrote something on it. Later, he left it in his office. Then he walked home – but to the old address. Suddenly he remembered. "Ah yes, a new house, a new address. Damn, where's that piece of paper?" But of course he couldn't find it. Then he looked around and saw a little girl. "Little girl," he said. "Do you know where the Hilberts live?"

[1] zerstreut

Ending 1: "I'm sorry, sir. They don't live here anymore."
Ending 2: "Yes, Dad. Mum sent me to find you. I'll take you home now."
Ending 3: "Yes, sir. But they don't like visitors."

The Story of the Stones 5 It's you!

1 **How well do you remember Episode 4? Circle T *(True)* or F *(False)*.**

1 Daniel thinks Darkman is trying to kill them.	T / F
2 Darkman attacked Gillian on the beach.	T / F
3 Gillian hit Darkman with her bag.	T / F
4 Gillian doesn't want to join the team.	T / F
5 Gillian is going to meet Sunborn.	T / F

2 **Look at the picture. Who do you think says:**

1 "Hello Gillian. And welcome to the team."
2 "Do you know where he is?"
3 "How about a wolf?"
4 "Isn't there a stone for me?"
5 "Darkman is very close."

3 **Watch Episode 5. Complete the sentences with the words in the box. There are some words you don't need.**

wolf	snake	Darkman	kill	Gillian
Sunborn	an alien	Emma	Daniel	Darkman

1 Darkman is trying to .... the children.
2 Gillian wants to be a ....
3 Gillian is really ....
4 .... kills ....

Everyday English

4 **Watch Episode 5 again. Complete the sentences.**

hopefully it wasn't your fault that's for sure Not exactly

a

Sunborn Yes. Hello, Gillian. And welcome to the team. We're happy to have you, [1] ....

b

Daniel Do you know where he is?
Sunborn [2] .... , but he's close.

c

Emma … but you didn't know that *we* brought him here.
Sunborn No, I didn't. But [3] .... – and you've helped me again.
Sarah And [4] .... for the last time!

Writing *for your Portfolio*

■ (13) **Work in pairs. Write down five things you *must* or *mustn't* do in school. Then get together with another pair and compare your list.**

Example:
We must be at school at eight o'clock.
We mustn't throw paper out of the window.

Grammar

SbX

like (doing)

So sagst du, dass jemand etwas gerne macht:
I **like** juggl**ing**.
They **like** roller-skating.
She **doesn't like** work**ing** out.

Complete. Write in the right order ing / like / person.
Bildung: [1] .... + [2] .... + [3] ....

SbX

mustn't

So sagst du, dass jemand etwas nicht tun darf oder etwas nicht geschehen darf.
Bildung: person + *mustn't (must not)* + *base form* des Verbs

You **mustn't** be home later than 8 o'clock.
We **mustn't** forget mum's birthday.

UNIT 13 Magic

1 CD 3 MP3 SbX

1 Listen to the poem. Then read it and put the pictures in the correct order.

Welcome

Welcome, welcome
to our school.
What you learn here
is quite cool.
How to pass through
walls and doors.
How to float
above the floors.
How to rattle
rusty chains.
How to make
a lot of stains.
How to scream
out in the night
How to take
your head off right.
Welcome, welcome
to our school,
what you learn here
is quite cool.

Time for a sketch

2 CD 3 MP3 SbX

2 Listen and read.

The school for young ghosts

It's the first day at school for the young ghosts.

Teacher Good evening.
Ghosts Ooooooooooooooooooooh.
Teacher Welcome to our school. On your first night I'm going to teach you …
Ghost 1 About castles in Britain?
Teacher No, that's next week.
Tonight you're going to learn how to pass through walls.
Ghost 2 And doors?
Teacher Yes, of course.

Ghost 3 But we can open doors easily.
Teacher Be quiet, you silly ghost! Passing through locked doors, of course.
Ghost 3 Sorry, sir.
Ghost 4 Do we learn how to scream loudly too?
Teacher Not this year. That's in year three.
Ghost 5 What about scaring people?
Teacher That's next month.
Ghost 6 I want to learn how to take my head off.
Teacher That's in year two. Tonight you're going to learn how to pass through walls. OK?
Ghost 6 Is it difficult to learn?
Teacher Passing through a wall can be difficult. Sometimes ghosts get stuck.
Ghost 7 I know, sir. My aunt got stuck in a wall when I was a baby. She's still there.
Teacher The poor woman!
Ghosts Oooooooooooooooh!
Teacher Be quiet! Now, you have to walk quietly. You mustn't say a word.
Ghost 8 Can I rattle my chains?
Teacher Aren't you listening? You have to walk quietly. No rattling.
Ghost 7 Fast or slowly?
Teacher Don't walk too fast and don't walk too slowly. I'll show you.
Ghosts Yes, please.
Teacher OK, watch me ...

Ghost 6 Where's the teacher now?
Ghost 5 In the wall. He got stuck.
Ghosts Hurray! What a great first lesson!

3 Circle T *(True)* or F *(False)*.

1 It's the first day at school for the young ghosts.	T / F
2 Today they are learning about castles in Britain.	T / F
3 They learn how to pass through walls and doors.	T / F
4 In year three, they learn how to scream loudly.	T / F
5 This year they also learn how to scare people.	T / F
6 Passing through a wall is very easy for a ghost.	T / F
7 A ghost mustn't walk quietly through a wall.	T / F
8 A ghost must walk through a wall very slowly.	T / F
9 The teacher gets stuck in the wall.	T / F

3 CD 3

4 Listen to the sketch again and act it out.

WB p. 80

Vocabulary

4 CD 3 SbX ■

5 Listen and then work in pairs.
You point to the picture, your partner says the word.

car boot
nail
put a spell on someone
feather
roast potatoes
fence
cooker
deckchair
sprinkle
prison

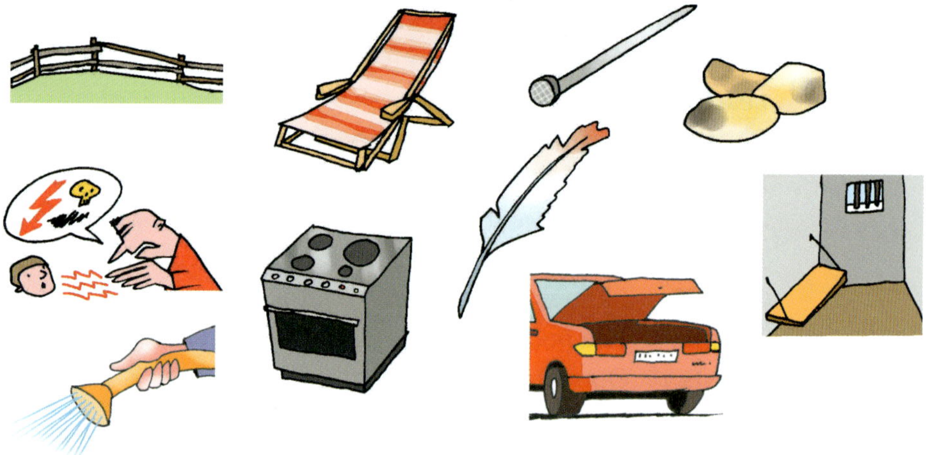

Story time

5 CD 3 MP3 ★

6 Read the story. Then listen to it.

Abracadabra, one, two, three

Debbie and her brother Robert were playing ball behind the house. Suddenly the ball landed in their neighbour's garden. "I'll get it," said Robert. "Be careful," Debbie said, "Mr Blogg loves to eat children for lunch." Robert didn't laugh. Mr Blogg was very unfriendly and Robert was scared of him. Slowly and quietly, Robert climbed over the fence. He looked through the bushes. The ball was right behind Mr Blogg's deckchair. Then everything happened very fast. Mr Blogg got up and shouted: "This time I'll get you!" Robert quickly climbed back over the fence. After a minute something came flying through the air. Robert and Debbie looked at it. "That was our ball," Robert said quietly. There was a big nail in the ball.

The following Saturday was Debbie's thirteenth birthday. They had a party in the garden with lots of friends. The young people were having a lot of fun. Suddenly Robert and Debbie's dad came into the garden. "Mr Blogg was here," he said. "You're making too much noise. Come into the house." The young people walked angrily into the house.
"Can we go out later and roast some potatoes over a fire?" Debbie asked.
"Of course," said her dad, "but don't make any noise."
An hour later they went out to roast the potatoes. They were very quiet, but after ten minutes they heard the doorbell. It was

Mr Blogg. Then dad came into the garden and told them to put out the fire.
"Mr Blogg says there is

▶ WB p. 81 ▶ CYBER HOMEWORK 25

too much smoke," he said. "I really don't like Mr Blogg," said Debbie.
Three days later Debbie and Robert were looking for Snowy, their cat. They found her under the bushes near the fence. Snowy was very ill. Robert also found a rotten fish. "We didn't have fish this week," said Debbie. "I'm sure Mr Blogg threw the fish over the fence." They carried the cat into the house.
"Poor Snowy," said Debbie, "I really don't like Mr Blogg."

The next day Debbie was in the garden with a book. "What are you reading?" Robert asked.
"It's a book on magic," said Debbie. "Sally gave it to me."
"What are you reading that for?" asked Robert.
"I want to put a spell on Mr Blogg."
"Spells don't work," said Robert.
"Do you want to help me or not?" asked Debbie.
"OK," said Robert. "What do I have to do?"
"The book says that we have to get five things from Mr Blogg," answered Debbie.
"We can do that easily," said Robert.

At ten o'clock that night, Debbie and Robert climbed the fence into Mr Blogg's garden. They found a feather, the rest of a cigar, a piece of bread, half a hot dog and a bottle of beer that was half full. They climbed back into their garden, put all the things in a pot and hid it in the garden shed. The next day they put the pot on the cooker and filled it with water. They cut up the feather, the rest of the cigar, the piece of bread, the rest of the hot dog and threw it in the water together with the beer. Then they filled an empty bottle of orange juice with the brown stuff.
"What do you want to do now?" Robert asked.
"We have to go into Mr Blogg's garden and sprinkle this stuff round his house."

They went over to the fence and listened carefully. Nothing. They climbed over and started to sprinkle the brown stuff. When Robert and Debbie got to the garage they stopped. The door of the garage was open and they could see Mr Blogg by his car. He was putting boxes into the boot. When he saw Debbie and Robert, he shouted: "Now I've got you." Debbie and Robert ran as fast as they could.

When they climbed the fence Robert lost one of his trainers. Mr Blogg picked it up.

"I'll show it to your dad when he comes home," he shouted. Then he got into his car and went away. "What can we do now?" asked Robert. "Dad's going to be very angry." "Let's go into town and see grandma," said Debbie. "We can have dinner with her. And when we get back, everything will be over."

When they arrived at grandma's place they phoned their mum. "We'll be back after dinner," Debbie said. After dinner grandma brought them back in her car. There was a police car in front of Mr Blogg's house. Debbie and Robert went over and talked to a policeman. "Mr Blogg had an accident in town," the police officer said. "Is he in hospital?" asked Debbie. "No, he's in prison because we found lots of stolen computers in the boot of his car. And the house is also full of stolen things." "So your spell worked," said Robert. "Yes, it did," said Debbie. "But I'm glad he isn't in hospital."

★ **7 Match the sentence halves.**

1 Robert threw the ball
2 Mr Blogg put a big nail
3 On Debbie's birthday they had a party
4 Debbie and Robert found their cat under
5 Debbie wanted to put a
6 When Debbie and Robert sprinkled the brown stuff in Mr Blogg's garden,
7 When Debbie and Robert came home there
8 The police found stolen computers in

☐ in the garden.
☐ the bushes near the fence.
☐ Mr Blogg's car and put him in prison.
☐ into the neighbour's garden.
☐ was a police car in front of Mr Blogg's house.
☐ into the ball.
☐ spell on Mr Blogg.
☐ he saw them.

6 CD 3 ■ **8 Listen to the interview with Julia and complete the information.**

Three reasons Julia likes *Charmed* ....

....

Who is her favourite character, and why? ....

The series is from ....

■ **9 Read the text and finish the sentences.**

"What can we do?" said a ghost. "We must help our teacher," said the smallest ghost. He gave his chains to another ghost. He walked to the wall. "Don't walk too slowly and don't walk too fast," the other ghosts shouted. So the smallest ghost began to walk slowly and quietly through the wall. In the wall, he took the teacher's hand and they both went through the wall. "Hurray!" all the young ghosts shouted and they rattled their chains loudly. "Thank you very much," the teacher said to the smallest ghost. "That's alright," said the smallest ghost.

1 The smallest ghost wanted …
2 He gave his chains …
3 Then he started to …
4 In the wall he took …
5 They both went …
6 The teacher thanked …

Writing *for your Portfolio*

★ **10 Look at the pictures and write the story.**

The teacher [1] ....
He put the [2] .... neck.
Then he [3] ....
All the young [4] ....

▶ WB p. 82

SbX

Grammar Adverbs of manner

Mit dem Adverb der Art und Weise drückst du aus, **wie** jemand etwas macht oder **wie** etwas geschieht.

Young ghosts learn how to scream **loudly**.
You have to walk **quietly**.
You mustn't walk too **slowly**.
Robert climbed back **quickly** over the fence.
The young people walked **angrily** into the house.
They climbed over the fence and listened **carefully**.
We can do that **easily**.

Bildung: Adjektiv + *ly*
quiet – quiet**ly**
quick – quick**ly**
slow – slow**ly**
careful – careful**ly**

Bei den Adjektiven, die auf *y* enden, wird das *y* zu einem *i*:
easy – eas**ily**
happy – happ**ily**
angry – angr**ily**

Annabel jumped quickly over the fence.

Ausnahmen:
fast – **fast** Don't walk too **fast**.
good – **well** I'm glad that it worked so **well**.

Complete with adverb or adjective.
Mit Hilfe eines [1] .... kannst du ein Nomen beschreiben.
Mit Hilfe eines [2] .... kannst du ein Verb beschreiben.

MORE fun with Fido!

UNIT 14 Where we live

SbX

1 Read. Match the texts to the photographs.

1 Mickey lives in a trailer park in Nebraska, USA. It's a place where motor homes and caravans can park, for a day, a week, a month, or for years! You can drive in, connect your home to the electricity, water and so on – and you're at home.

2 Shirley lives in a flat on the 15th floor of a building in Britain. But there aren't fifteen floors of flats – the first 3 floors are the garages for the people's cars!!

3 Shania lives in a house in New Mexico, USA. It's very modern, but it's also very unusual. The house was built from old car tyres, aluminium tins and earth! It's called an 'Earthship'. All the heat comes from solar panels in the roof.

4 Teresa lives in the north of England, in a bungalow. Teresa's bungalow has got three bedrooms and a large garden – and that's why she loves living there!

5 Jake's family has got a very different house – it's in a tree! The house is near San Diego, in California. But this isn't the place that they live in all the time. The family also have a flat in San Diego – they go to the tree house at the weekends.

2 Read again and answer.

1 Who lives above garages?
2 Who's got a large garden?
3 Whose family has got more than one place to live?
4 Who lives in a house made from old tyres?
5 Who lives in a house that can move to other places?

Vocabulary Inside a room

7 CD 3 SbX

3 **Write the numbers next to the words. Then listen and check.**

◯ wardrobe	◯ fridge	◯ sink	◯ radiator
◯ bed	◯ cooker	◯ cupboard	◯ sofa
◯ table	◯ bedside table	◯ carpet	◯ curtains
◯ chair	◯ armchair	◯ rug	◯ lamp

Get talking Memory game

4 **In pairs. One of you closes your book. Test each other!**

A What colour's the table?

B It's …

A That's right. / No, it's …

Sounds right /juː/ /ʊ/

8 CD 3 MP3

5 **Listen and say the poem.**

New curtains for the window,
new cupboards for my books.
A wardrobe for my clothes, and
how nice my bedroom looks!

Get talking Remembering

● 6 **Look at the plan of the house. Close your book. Say what's in each room.**

living room
kitchen
bathroom
Mike and Nick's room
Joanna's room

In the living room, there's a television, and …
In the kitchen, there are …

9 CD 3

7 **Listen. Which room are the people in?**

Conversation 1: ....
Conversation 2: ....
Conversation 3: ....
Conversation 4: ....

10 CD 3

8 **Listen again and complete. Use the words in the box.**

mine
yours
hers
his
whose
ours
theirs
whose

Mum [1] .... school bag is this?
Mike It's Joanna's.
Mum Well, it shouldn't be on the sofa. Take it to her room, please.
Mike Why me? It's [2] .... , not [3] ....!

Simon I like your room.
Nick Thanks. I share it with my brother. This is my bed, and that's [4] ....
Simon Right. Is this your computer?
Nick Yes and no – I mean, it's [5] ....!

Mum [6] .... trainers are those? Are they [7] ....?
Joanna No – they're Mike's! I borrowed them, and they got dirty – so now I'm cleaning them.
Mum OK – but don't clean them here, in the bathroom! Wash them in the kitchen!

Mike Mum – why is there a dictionary here on the fridge?
Mum Oh, that – yes, can you take it to Mr and Mrs Smith next door, please?
Mike OK. Is it [8] ....?
Mum No, it's ours, but they want to borrow it.

11 CD 3 MP3

9 Listen. Then act out the dialogue.

Susan Whose camera is this? Is it yours?
Mark No. It's hers.

10 Act out more dialogues. Think of other things to mime.

12 CD 3 MP3

11 Listen and complete. Then say the chant together.

Whose is it? Is it yours?
No, it isn't [1] ....
Whose is it? Is it Mike's?
No, it isn't [2] ....
Whose is it? Is it Sue's?
No, it isn't [3] ....
Whose is it? Jane and Paul's?
No, it isn't [4] ....

Whose is it? Whose is it?
Give it to us.
It's ours!
And it's so good!
Mmm!

Writing *for your Portfolio*

12 Read Emily's text and answer the questions.

1 Which is her favourite room? **2 Why does Emily like this room best?**

The best place in my house.

The best place in my house is the kitchen. There's a big table and four chairs where we have breakfast and dinner. There's a big window and we can look into the garden. There's a sink and a fridge, but not a washing machine (that's in the garage). Our cat's basket is in the kitchen, too, and she sleeps there at night.
I like the kitchen because it's a place for all the family. It's always warm in there, too!

13 Write one of these texts.

a) The best place in my house **b)** My ideal room

WB p. 87

The Story of the Stones 6 Farewell!

1 Use the pictures to tell the story of Episode 5.

2 What do you think happens to these in the final episode?

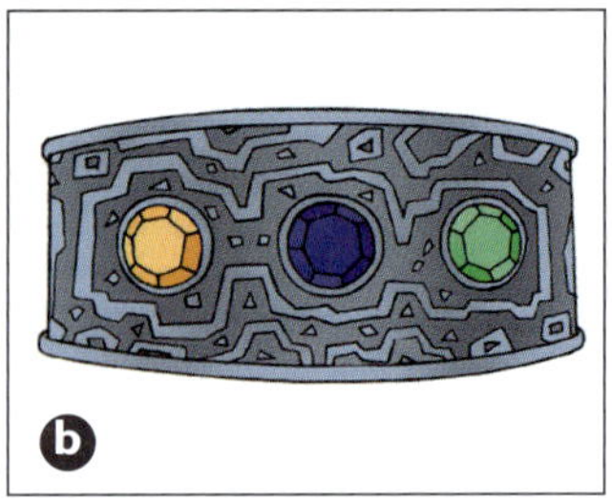

3 Watch Episode 6 and answer the questions.

1 Why does Sunborn destroy the belt and stones?
2 What happens when she destroys the belt and stones?
3 What can the children no longer do?

4 Complete the sentences about you.

1 My favourite character in 'The story of the stones' is ....
because ....
2 My least favourite character in 'The story of the stones' is ....
because ....
3 My favourite scene was ....

Everyday English

5 Watch Episode 6 again. Complete the sentences with the words in the box and match the questions and answers.

I'm afraid so	believe me	it doesn't matter	I'm afraid not

1 But not everything is over yet.
2 So we can't morph any longer?
3 Does this mean we won't see you again?
4 Can't you stay here?

☐ That's right, Daniel. But [1].......... .
☐ [2].......... . There's no place for me here on Earth.
☐ The Lord of the Fire still lives. He won't give up, [3].......... .
☐ [4].......... , Sarah. But I'll never forget you.

Grammar

SbX

Whose ... ?

Wenn du fragen willst, wem etwas gehört, fragst du mit *Whose ... ?*

Whose school bag is this? **Whose** trainers are those?

SbX

Possessive 's

Wenn du sagen willst, wem etwas gehört, hängst du an den Namen der Person oder das Nomen *'s* an:

Whose bag is this? It's **Joanna's**. They're **Mike's** trainers.
This is **my brother's** bed.

Wenn der Name oder das Nomen im Plural steht, setzt du ans Ende des Wortes ein ' (Apostroph):

This is my **parents'** room. It's our **neighbours'** dog.

Bei Wörtern mit unregelmäßiger Pluralform setzt du *'s* ans Ende des Wortes:

That's the **children's** school. Don't take other **people's** things!

SbX

Possessive pronouns

Du verwendest ein *possessive pronoun*, wenn du sagen willst, wem etwas gehört – ohne dass du den Namen der Person verwendest.

Complete. Write *he/I/they/she* in the spaces.

(1................) It's **mine**.
(you) Are they **yours**?
(2................) This is my bed, and that's **his**.
(3................) The bag is **hers**.
(we) The computer is **ours**.
(4................) The dictionary isn't **theirs**.

UNIT 15 Feeling better

Story time

13 CD 3 MP3 SbX

1 **Read the story. Then listen to it.**

The pink pill

On Monday morning Mr Wilkins went to the doctor's.
"Hello Mr Wilkins and how are you today?" asked the doctor. The doctor knew his name because Mr Wilkins visited him so often.
"I'm not feeling very well, doctor." said Mr Wilkins. "I've got a headache."
"Oh dear," said the doctor and he gave Mr Wilkins a yellow pill. "Take this and go to bed. Tomorrow you'll be fine."
Mr Wilkins looked a bit disappointed. "My friend told me about the pink pill," he said to the doctor. "He said it's great for headaches."
The doctor smiled at Mr Wilkins. "I told you last week," he said. "The pink pill is only for people who are very ill."
Mr Wilkins left the doctor's.
He wasn't very happy.

—•—

The next morning Mr Wilkins went to the doctor's again.
"I've still got a headache," he told the doctor. "But now I've got a pain in my arm as well."
"Oh dear," said the doctor and he gave Mr Wilkins a green pill. "Take this and go to bed. Tomorrow, you'll be fine."
Mr Wilkins was a bit disappointed. "What about the pink pill?" he asked. "My friend said it's excellent when your arm hurts."
The doctor just smiled and said "Goodbye."

—•—

On Wednesday Mr Wilkins went to the doctor's again.
"I've still got a headache and a pain in my arm," he told the doctor. "But now my leg hurts as well."
"Oh dear," said the doctor and he gave Mr Wilkins a blue pill. "Take this and go to bed. Tomorrow, you'll be fine."
"And the pink pill?" Mr Wilkins asked. "My friend says it's perfect when your leg hurts."
The doctor just smiled and said "Goodbye."

—•—

On Thursday morning Mr Wilkins ran quickly to the doctor's.
"Hello Mr Wilkins," said the doctor. "Do you feel better today?"
"No doctor. I feel terrible," said Mr Wilkins.
"Oh dear, what's the matter?" asked the doctor.
"I've still got a headache and my arm and my leg still hurt. But now I've got earache as well. Oh doctor, I'm in so much pain," said Mr Wilkins.
"You know what?" the doctor said to Mr Wilkins. "It's time for the pink pill!" Mr Wilkins took the pill, put it in his mouth and smiled for the first time in a week.

Mr Wilkins left the doctor's and went out into the street. He was so happy that he didn't see the man on the bike. The man shouted "Watch out!" but it was too late.

When Mr Wilkins opened his eyes, the doctor was speaking to him from the window. "Would you like another pink pill?" he asked. Mr Wilkins jumped up and ran away. "No thank you!" he shouted. "No more pink pills!"

SbX

2 **Write the names of the people under the pictures.**

....

Sue's got a pain in her ankle.
Tim's head hurts.
Jacob's knee hurts.
Emily's got a pain in her back.
William's throat hurts.
Jessica's got stomach ache.

Sounds right /p/ /b/ /æ/ /e/

14 CD 3 MP3

3 **Listen and repeat.**

A pain in your hand?
A pain in your back?
That's too bad!
A pain in your leg?
A pain in your head?
Then stay in bed!

Note:
I've got stomach ache.
(or stomachache).
I've got earache.
I've got toothache.
I've got backache.
But we usually say
'I've got **a** headache.'

Get talking Aches and pains

4 **Work in groups of three. Act out a problem and talk about it.**

WB p. 93

15 CD 3

5 **Listen and number the pictures in the order you hear them.**

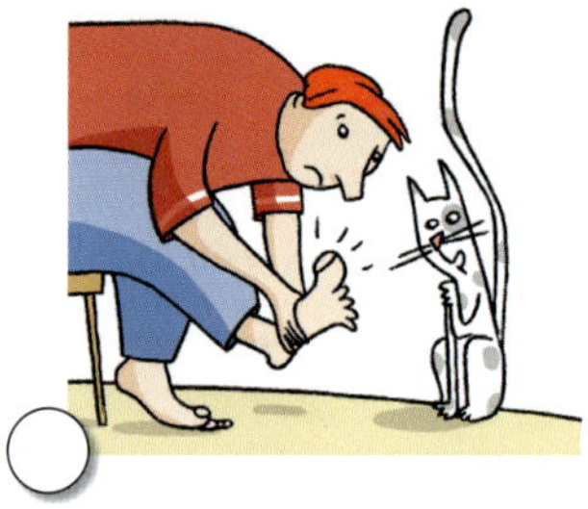

6 **Complete the dialogues with the words in the box. Practise the dialogues in pairs.**

dropped
cut
broken
walked
fallen
hurt

1 Does your head hurt?
Yes, I've just .... into a lamp post.

2 What's the matter?
I think I've .... my toe.

3 There's blood on your shirt.
Yes, I've just .... my hand.

4 Why is he walking like that?
He's .... his ankle.

5 Why is she crying?
She's just .... a heavy box on her foot.

6 Come quickly.
Why? What's the matter?
Kevin's .... out of the tree.

7 **Look at the conversations and find the past participles of these verbs. Write them.**

walk	break	cut	hurt	fall	drop
....	....	....	....	....	....

8 **Here are some more past participles. What do you think the base forms of the verbs are? Write them.**

eaten	loved	thought	hit	told	played
....	....	....	....	....	....
put	met	known	wanted	rung	read
....	....	....	....	....	....

WB p. 94
CYBER HOMEWORK 29

9 **Read the text about the Amazon.**

The world's new gold

The Amazon Rainforest is very important for our planet. It produces more than 20% of our oxygen[1]. But people cut down the trees and want to make money quickly.

Scientists have found lots of special plants in the Amazon Rainforest. These plants can help sick people. More than 2,000 plants in the Amazon Rainforest can help against cancer. And other plants can help against other illnesses. These plants are the world's new gold.

Five hundred years ago, more than 10,000,000 Indians lived in the Amazon Rainforest. Now there are less than 200,000. The Indian medicine men know a lot about these special plants. But many of the medicine men are now very old. It is important for the world that we learn what they know!

[1] Sauerstoff

10 **Circle T *(True)* or F *(False)*.**

1 The Amazon river produces 20% of our oxygen. T / F

2 People cut down lots of trees in the Amazon Rainforest. T / F

3 Scientists have found plants. These plants can help sick people. T / F

4 Scientists have found lots of gold in the Amazon Rainforest. T / F

5 Ten million Indians live in the Amazon Rainforest. T / F

6 There are 200,000 medicine men. T / F

16 CD 3 MP3

11 **Read and listen to the poem.**

An apple a day

An apple a day
keeps the doctor away.
Well, that's what they say
and it's true.

Drop it on his head
when he walks through the door,
and he won't come back
any more!

Writing *for your Portfolio*

12 **Read the letter and answer the questions.**

Dear Harry,
Miss Black has just told us about your accident.
So you fell off a horse and broke your ankle!
That's terrible! And now you have to stay at
home for three weeks. Three weeks with no
school – poor you! But don't worry – Miss Black
said she's going to send you lots of homework.
The big news is that the school football team won yesterday.
Now they're in the final. The game's on Saturday, so think about us.
We all miss you. Get well and come back soon!
Lots of love,
Your friends in class 8A.

1 What's the name of the class teacher?
2 What happened to Harry?
3 How long is he going to be away from school?
4 What is the teacher going to send him?
5 What is the big news?

★ **13** **Imagine one of your classmates is at home and can't come to school. Write him or her a letter. Think about the questions above to help you with ideas.**

WB p. 95

SbX

Grammar

Present perfect

Du verwendest das *present perfect*, um jemanden eine Neuigkeit zu erzählen. Dabei wird nicht erwähnt, wann dies geschehen ist.

I've **lost** my cat. We've **bought** a new car. She's **cut** her finger.
David **has broken** his leg. They've **gone** on holiday.

Wenn du betonen willst, dass etwas gerade geschehen ist, verwendest du *just*.
I've **just passed** my English test.
They've **just got** married.

They've just scored a goal.

Du bildest das *present perfect* mit dem *past participle* (der 3. Form) des Verbs.
He**'s fallen** off his bike.
We**'ve** just **moved** house.

Past participles

Das *past participle* findest du in der dritten Spalte der Verblisten. Bei regelmäßigen Verben hat das *past participle* die gleiche Form wie das *past*. Da hängst du an die Nennform *-ed* (oder *-d*) an.

pass	pass**ed**	pass**ed**
walk	walk**ed**	walk**ed**
move	mov**ed**	mov**ed**

Die Formen der unregelmäßigen Verben solltest du am besten auswendig lernen:

go	went	**gone**	lose	lost	**lost**
buy	bought	**bought**	cut	cut	**cut**
fall	fell	**fallen**	hurt	hurt	**hurt**
break	broke	**broken**	win	won	**won**

Kids in NYC 3

The city quiz

Before you watch

1 Write the words under the pictures.

an Internet café
a library
a prize
a quiz

1.................. 2.................. 3.................. 4..................

2 In what order do you think these pictures come in the DVD? Write 1–4 in the boxes.

A ☐

B ☐

C ☐

D ☐

Watch the story

3 Check your answers to 2.

4 Circle T *(True)* or F *(False)*.

1 The children have written a quiz.	T / F
2 There are 20 questions in the quiz.	T / F
3 The children can win a prize in the quiz.	T / F
4 The children have three hours to do the quiz.	T / F

5 Complete the dialogue.

with
idea
way
off
crazy
together

Jenny Come on – let's all do the quiz [1] ....

Gerry No [2] ....! I'm going to the Internet café over here. I'm going to get all my answers [3] .... the Internet.

Emma Great [4] ...., Gerry. Can I come [5] .... you?

Gerry Sure. We can get a coffee too.

Steve You're [6] .... What if the teacher sees you?

Gerry Ah! Who cares?

Jenny Come on, Steve. Let's start. Bye, you guys. See you at two!

6 Answer the questions.

1 What time do the children have to be back at the park?

....

2 What does Gerry order at the Internet café?

....

3 Which street is the New York Public Library on?

....

7 Complete the list of places that Steve and Jenny see.

St Patrick's Cathedral, …

Everyday English

8 Complete the dialogues.

Let's see
have fun
Who cares?
I have no clue.

Progress Check Units 11–15

Listening

17 CD 3

Listen to a dialogue between a boy, a girl and the boy's grandfather. Choose the correct answers.

1 The boy's grandfather is sleeping in …
2 The girl hurts her …
3 The boy wants to open …
4 Granddad's got …
5 Granddad's pills are …

☐ 5

Reading

Read the email. Circle *True* or *False*.

Hi Laura,
Guess what? We've just moved house! You know that before, we lived in that terrible block of flats. Well, now we live in a nice bungalow in Harpington. And the really good thing is, I've got my own bedroom now (and my sister has hers, too). It's got a wardrobe and curtains, and next week I'm going to get a carpet for it. So, I'm really happy.
My dad isn't very well today. He's got stomach ache. I think it's because he ate a lot of pumpkin pie last night. Well, I hope he gets better soon. Tomorrow, my uncle and aunt are coming to visit us in the new house, and dad mustn't be in bed when they come!
Please come and see me soon – you can sleep in my bedroom and see the new carpet!
Lots of love,
Jenny

1 Jenny doesn't live in a flat now.	T / F
2 Jenny and her sister sleep in the same bedroom.	T / F
3 There is a carpet in Jenny's bedroom.	T / F
4 Jenny's father's got stomach ache.	T / F
5 Jenny's family is going to visit her aunt and uncle tomorrow.	T / F

☐ 5

Grammar

Circle the correct answer.

1 Please don't walk so *slow / slowly.*
2 I love *go / going* to the cinema.
3 It's *Joanna's / Joanna* cat.
4 *Who / Whose* pencil is this?
5 Excuse me – are these shoes *yours / your*?
6 I *has / have* bought a new MP3-player.
7 He sings very *good / well.*
8 He isn't here – he *is / has* just gone out.
9 This computer is *my / mine.*
10 Who *does know / knows* the answer to this question?

☐ 10

Vocabulary

Write the words under the pictures.

a 
b 

c 
d 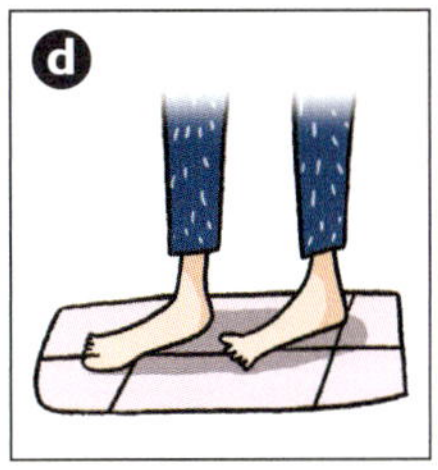
e 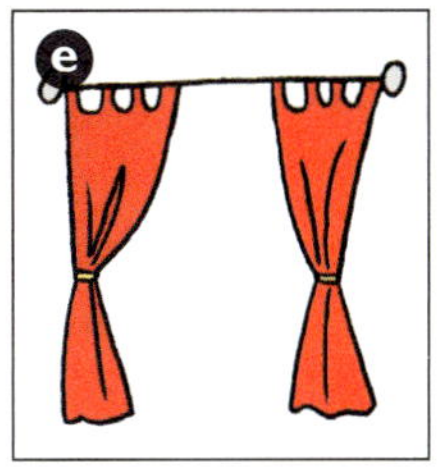

....

☐ 5

Dialogue

Tick the correct answers.

1 What's the matter?
☐ A I've got a headache.
☐ B It's mine.
☐ C No, it isn't.

2 Are these yours?
☐ A Yes, I am.
☐ B No, it's mine.
☐ C No, they're Mike's.

3 Whose dictionary is this?
☐ A It's English–German.
☐ B It's mine.
☐ C That's right.

4 Does it hurt?
☐ A Not very much.
☐ B That's too bad.
☐ C I can't remember.

5 What if the teacher sees us?
☐ A I haven't got a clue.
☐ B Here we go.
☐ C Who cares?

☐ 5

How did you do?

	☺	😐	☹
Listening	4-5	2-3	0-1
Reading	4-5	2-3	0-1
Grammar	7-10	4-6	0-3
Vocabulary	4-5	2-3	0-1
Dialogue	4-5	2-3	0-1
Total	21-30	11-20	0-10

▶ MORE! ONLINE PROGRESS CHECK - www.more-online.at

UNIT 16 Virtual worlds

SbX ■

1 **Read and match the pictures with the dialogues. There is one picture too many. Which is it?**

DIALOGUE 1

Lisa Have you seen the new *Goal!!!* football game?

Thomas Yeah. I've already played it a few times.

Lisa Is it any good?

Thomas It's brilliant. You can choose all your favourite players and create your own football team. And then you can go online and play against other people. You can even join an online league. But of course you don't have to. You can just play against the computer at home.

Lisa Sounds cool. Can I come around tomorrow?

Thomas Sure.

DIALOGUE 2

Natasha Hi Sonja. I've just played *Animal Rescue 3*. It's so cool.

Sonja Really? I haven't seen it yet. But I loved parts one and two.

Natasha I got it yesterday. I played until midnight and I got up at seven this morning to play more!

Sonja So what do you like about it?

Natasha Well this one's set in the African jungle so you have to find and rescue some really cool animals like gorillas, snakes and leopards.

Sonja Cool. Does it look good?

Natasha It's awesome. The graphics are the best I've ever seen. The animals and the jungle are so realistic. It's amazing.

Sonja It sounds great. I can't wait to play it.

DIALOGUE 3

Adrian What do you think of the new *Pirate Ahoy* game?

Fred I haven't played it yet. I'm playing another game at the moment.

Adrian Yeah, I've heard about that. Anyway, this new *Pirate Ahoy* game is brilliant. It's part action game and part strategy game. You play the part of Blackbeard and you have to …

Fred OK, OK. Don't tell me too much. I want to find out for myself. Let's meet tomorrow and play it.

▶ WB p. 100

Story time

18 CD 3 MP3 ★

2 **Read and listen to the play.**

gameworld.doc

(Janet, Julian and Ron are in a game group called The Weird World of Wakarimaska. *Wakarimaska is a fantasy gaming world. To go to this world you need a computer and a helmet. The Gamemasters give you roles. With luck and good play, you can change your roles. Working in teams is a good idea. That's why Janet, Julian and Ron often help each other. When the game came out in 2043, only about 800 people played it, but now, eight years later, there are nearly 30,000 players in* Wakarimaska.*)*

SCENE 1

Ron Hi, Julian. What's up?
Julian Ron, listen. I've just had two emails from Janet. She's in the Forest of Doom. She needs help. Somebody's following her, and she can't find out who it is. What are we going to do?
Ron I see. Look, come over to my place and we can check it out. Quickly – and don't forget to bring your helmet!

(Fifteen minutes later.)

Ron I've already logged in. Put your helmet on and let's go and look for Janet. She's in the Forest of Doom, and she's in danger.
Julian Right. We must help her, and now!

SCENE 2

Janet Thank God you're here. I've already tried to get out of Wakarimaska, but I can't. I don't know why. Maybe we can get out together.
Julian Why get out? We have to find out what's going on. Somebody very powerful is after you. And now the same person is after us. Maybe the person's trying to take us out of the game.

(Suddenly Ron heard a noise. He turned around and ran behind a rock.)

Janet Hey, what's going on? Ron, where are you?

(Ron came back with a small boy.)

Ron Look who I've found.
Colin Please let me go!
Janet Who are you? I haven't seen you before.
Colin My name's Colin, and I'm a servant at the castle. Please let me go!

Julian Let him go. He looks harmless. We've got other problems. Someone's trying to hurt us. We have to find him – or her.

Colin Maybe I can help.

Janet You? How?

Colin Well, I saw a strange woman in the forest half an hour ago. She was very tall, and she had long black hair and very blue eyes. When she saw me, she ran into a cave.

Janet Can you find that cave again?

Colin Yes, I'm sure I can.

Ron Then let's go.

(A few minutes later.)

Colin Here's the cave. She went in here.

Julian Right, let's go in. Colin, you go first, then me, then Ron and Janet. And let's be very quiet and very careful.

Ron Hang on, Janet. I want to leave a sign outside so people know that the cave's important. I'll be back in a minute. Wait for me.

(Ron quickly ran back and then went into the cave. Only Colin was there.)

Ron Where are Julian and Janet?

Colin They've already gone to the next part of the cave. Come on, follow me.

(Suddenly, Ron knew that something wasn't right. 'Why didn't they wait?' he thought. 'Janet knew about my plan.' He looked at Colin. Colin looked different. He didn't look like a boy any longer. His hair was long and black now – and then Ron understood. He turned and ran. He ran and ran until he was at the portal to the real world – and suddenly he was in his chair again. Julian was next to him. Ron took off his helmet and tried to wake Julian up, but he couldn't. He took Julian's helmet off, but he still didn't wake up.)

SCENE 3

Ron Julian, Julian! Come on, wake up! OK, I have to phone the Gamemasters.

Woman Gamemasters service desk. Can I help you?

Ron Yes, please, it's very important. I've just come back into the real world with a friend, but I can't wake him up. A group of friends are still in the Forest of Doom. I don't know what's going on.

Woman Right. Five other players have already had this problem. It's very serious. Somebody is trying to get control of *Wakarimaska*. Tell me where you live, and we'll send somebody to help you.

(Ron gave her his address. He went back and tried to wake Julian again. Then the doorbell rang. Ron ran to the door and opened it.)

Ron Thank God you're here! I'm so worried. I … but, but …

(Ron looked at the woman. She was tall, with long black hair, and very blue eyes.)

Woman Hello, Ron. Thank you for phoning me. I'm the future queen of *Wakarimaska*.

★ **3** **Circle T (*True*) or F (*False*).**

1 In 2043 thousands of people played the *Wakarimaska* game.	T / F
2 Janet was in the Forest of Doom without her friends.	T / F
3 Janet thinks that a wizard is following her.	T / F
4 Julian and Ron think that something very powerful is in the Forest of Doom.	T / F
5 Colin says he wants to help them.	T / F
6 Colin doesn't want to go into the cave.	T / F
7 Ron left *The Weird World of Wakarimaska.*	T / F
8 Ron phoned the Gamemasters and asked for help.	T / F
9 A friendly woman came to help him.	T / F
10 Janet and Julian came back from *Wakarimaska.*	T / F

19 CD 3

4 **Listen to what the following people say about video and PC games and answer the questions below.**

Interview with Jonathan

1 Does Jonathan often play games?
2 What kind of games does he like?

Interview with Sharon

1 What does Sharon think of the *Middle Earth* games?
2 Why can't she use the computer all the time?

Interview with Mr Sutton

1 Why does Mr Sutton not like computer games?
2 Does he buy games for his children?

Interview with Mrs Frampton

1 Why does Mrs Frampton say 'No' to some games?
2 What does she tell parents about games when they ask her?

WB p. 101 CYBER HOMEWORK 31

Get talking Asking for information

■ **5** **Work in pairs. Ask your partner about a video game or a PC game.**

A Have you played ....?
B No, I haven't. Have you?
A Yes, I have.
B Is it good?
A Yeah. The graphics are awesome!

A Have you played ....?
B Yes, I've already played it five times.
A What's it like?
B It's OK. But the real fun is when you go online!

Writing *for your Portfolio*

6 **Do one of the tasks.**

SbX

a) Write about your favourite game.

My favourite game is Ratchet & Clank 3. In this game you're on the planet Veldin. You have to fight Dr. Nefarious, who wants to kill all life on the planet. Together with Captain Quark and the Q-Force, you fight on four levels. The best thing is the multiplayer mode. Four people can play offline, but you can also go online, and then eight players can play. It's great fun!

b) Write why you (don't) like playing video games.

● Text 1
I don't like video games. I think they're boring. Most of the time you just try to kill some creatures. I don't see what's so good about that. Or you race around in cars or on motorbikes. I like watching TV and reading books.

■ Text 2
I like playing video games. For some games you have to be very clever and have good ideas. And I like playing these games with my friends very much. I ask them round, and we have a good time. After school, this is a great way to have fun and to talk to your friends, too.

Sounds right /v/ /w/

20 CD 3 MP3

7 Listen and repeat.

Very easy video games
are very often fun.
When we played one yesterday
my brother Willy won!!

SbX

Grammar Present perfect with *already* and *yet*

Zur Erinnerung: Du verwendest das *present perfect* oft dann, wenn du nicht über einen bestimmten Zeitpunkt in der Vergangenheit sprichst.
I**'ve heard** about it. (= Ich weiß davon, jemand hat mir irgendwann davon erzählt.)
She**'s gone** home. (= Sie ist nicht hier, sie ist irgendwann nach Hause gegangen.)

Wenn du sagen willst, dass jemand etwas schon gemacht hat, kannst du das *present perfect* mit dem Wort *already* verwenden. Das Wort *already* kommt zwischen *has/have* und dem *past participle* (3. Form des Verbs).
I**'ve already logged** in.
They**'ve already gone** to the next part of the cave.
Some other players **have already had** this problem.

Wenn du sagen willst, dass etwas noch nicht geschehen ist, verwendest du *not yet* mit *present perfect*. Das Wort *yet* kommt an das Satzende.
I **haven't played** it **yet.**
There's a new film at the cinema, but I **haven't seen** it **yet.**

WB pp. 102, 103 CYBER HOMEWORK 32

Caring for animals

Vocabulary Looking after your pet

21 CD 3 SbX

1 Listen and fill in numbers.

stroke your pet

play with your pet

feed your pet

clean out the cage

walk your pet

brush your pet

give your pet a bath

dry your pet

clean out the litter tray

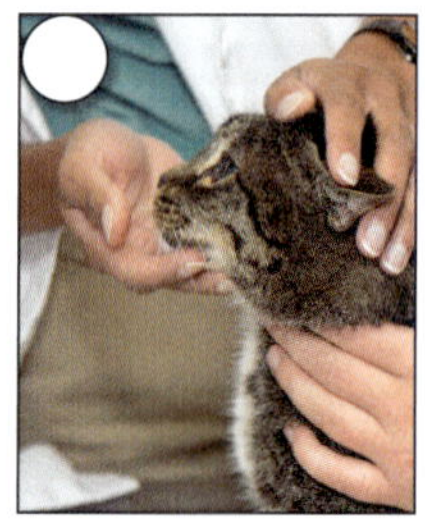
take your pet to the vet

2 Play a memory game.

A What did you do yesterday?

B 5, 2, 9.

A Ah, you fed your pet, you walked your pet and you took your pet to the vet.

B That's right.

22 CD 3 SbX

3 Listen to the interviews and tick.

Megan

What is Megan's pet?	☐ a cat	☐ a hamster	☐ a dog
What colour is she?	☐ black and white	☐ black and grey	☐ black, grey and brown
Where does she sleep?	☐ in Megan's room	☐ in the bathroom	☐ in the living room
How often does she feed her?	☐ once a day	☐ twice a day	☐ three times a day
How much time a day does she spend on her?	☐ 15 minutes	☐ 50 minutes	☐ 90 minutes

David

What is David's pet?	☐ a cat	☐ a hamster	☐ a dog
What colour is he?	☐ black	☐ brown	☐ brown and white
Where does he sleep?	☐ in the hall	☐ in David's room	☐ in the living room
How often does he feed him?	☐ once a day	☐ twice a day	☐ three times a day
How much time a day does he spend on him?	☐ 15 minutes	☐ 50 minutes	☐ 90 minutes

23 CD 3

4 Listen to the interviews again and complete the sentences.

1 Megan doesn't often …
2 When Megan does her homework her cat …
3 Megan doesn't like to …
4 When it rains David has to …
5 David's sister doesn't …
6 David plays a lot with Buddy when he …

Get talking Asking about pets

5 Hold interviews. Ask two classmates. Take notes.

A Have you got a pet?
B Yes, I have.
A What is it?
B A mouse.
A What colour is it?
B …
A How often do you feed it?
B …

A Have you got a pet?
B No, I haven't.
A What would you like?
B A dog.
A Where does it sleep?
B …
A How much time a day do you spend on it?
B …

6 Report to the class.

Nathalie has got a … . It's … . It sleeps … . She feeds it … . She spends … minutes on it.

WB p. 106 CYBER HOMEWORK 33

Time for a sketch

24 CD 3 MP3 SbX

7 **Listen and read. Two dogs, Rover and Wallace, are talking.**

Small talk between dogs

Wallace Hi Rover. How are you?
Rover Oh, hi Wallace. Fine, thanks. And you?
Wallace I'm very busy at the moment. I have to walk my owner twice a day.
Rover Really? Why's that?
Wallace He's getting a bit fat. So I walk him twice a day for an hour. And as soon as we get to the park here, I run away from him as fast as I can. Then he has to run, too! Of course I only do that to keep him fit.

Rover Great idea!
Wallace Do you like the park?
Rover Oh, yes. I've got lots of friends here.
Wallace So have I. There's only one dog around that I don't like much: Admiral. He thinks he can boss everybody around. I really don't like him.
Rover Neither do I. And he wants to fight all the time. I hate that.
Wallace So do I.
Rover By the way, are you here alone today?
Wallace No, I'm not. But I ran up this hill so fast that my owner couldn't follow me. Here he comes now. And he's shouting my name again. I don't like it when owners shout!

Rover	Neither do I. Owners are a pain! Mine's very strange, too.
Wallace	Oh? Why?
Rover	Well, I have to watch TV with her. And she wants to stroke me all the time while she's watching. She thinks I like it, you know! But I hate it when she strokes me. And I hate TV. I haven't seen a good programme for a long time.
Wallace	Neither have I. Yesterday I had to watch a programme for pet owners. Very boring! All about how to teach your dog how to behave! And another thing – my owner always takes me for rides in his car. But he's such a bad driver. I always get a headache in the car.
Rover	Yeah, I know. Life isn't always easy.
Wallace	Sorry Rover, I've got to go. He's shouting again. I just don't understand humans!

■ **8** **Circle T *(True)* or F *(False)*.**

1 Wallace has to go for walks with his owner twice a day.	T / F
2 Wallace is getting fat.	T / F
3 Wallace likes the park, but Rover doesn't like it.	T / F
4 Wallace and Rover don't like Admiral.	T / F
5 Admiral wants to fight all the time. Wallace likes that.	T / F
6 Wallace hasn't seen a good TV programme for a long time.	T / F

WB p. 107

★ **9** **Read the text.**

Where horses can live in peace

Rocky Mount is a small town of about 5,000 people in the state of Virginia in the US. It's a quiet and beautiful place, not far from the Blue Ridge Mountains.

Rocky Mount is also the home of the Dream Catcher Farm Horse Sanctuary. It's a place where horses can live peacefully. But can't all horses live in peace? No. Some owners don't look after their horses very well, or don't care for them and don't give them enough food. Some people don't want their horses any more because they're old. The people at the Dream Catcher Farm Horse Sanctuary believe that all creatures should live free from cruelty. That's why they have created this place for horses.

One of the horses they have saved is Rocky. For 3 years, Rocky had to stay in a small stable. He got very little food and water, and was very ill when the people from the Horse Sanctuary heard about him. At the Horse Sanctuary, Rocky got hay, water and love. A very good vet looked after him. Seven months later, he was OK again. Now Rocky is a healthy, happy horse, thanks to the people from the Dream Catcher Farm Horse Sanctuary.

Rocky 7 months ago.

Now he's healthy and happy.

★ **10** **Answer the questions.**

1 How many people live in Rocky Mount?
2 How do some owners treat their horses badly?
3 Why don't some people want their horses?
4 What was the problem for Rocky?
5 How long did it take for Rocky to be OK again?
6 How is Rocky now?

▶ WB p. 108

Writing *for your Portfolio*

11 Read the texts. Then write your own text.

■ Text 1

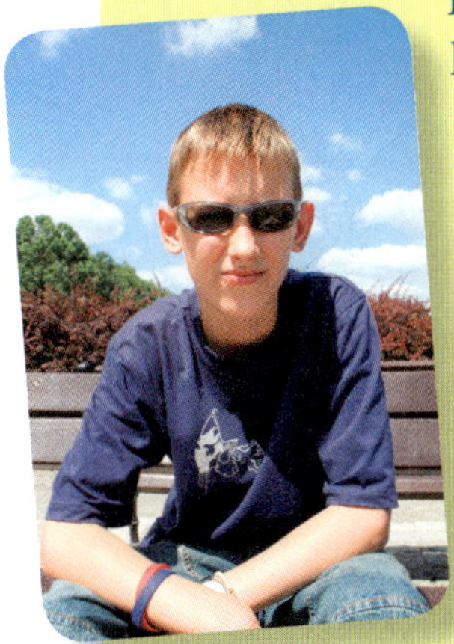

I haven't got a pet. We live in a flat and my parents always say "no". I'd like a dog. My parents say dogs are a lot of work, but I don't think so. One of my friends has got a dog. He doesn't spend a lot of time on it. We sometimes play with it in the park.

★ Text 2

My pet is a rat. He's brown and his name is Fluff. I often play with Fluff. He likes it when I put him inside my shirt. Some of my friends are scared of Fluff. When I take Fluff out of my shirt or jacket, they run away. I don't understand that. I clean the cage every second day and I put in clean water twice every day. At night Fluff sleeps in a cage. When I get up at the weekend, I put him in the pocket of my pyjamas. Then I go into the kitchen and hug my mum. When she feels Fluff, she screams.

SbX

Grammar *So (do/have) I. / Neither (do/have) I.*

Read the examples. Complete the sentences with *neither* and *so*.

A "I **like** the park."
B "**So do** I." (= ich auch.)
A "I really **don't** like him."
B "**Neither do** I."
(= Ich auch nicht.)

A "I**'ve** got lots of friends here."
B "So **have** I." (= ich auch.)
A "I **haven't seen** a good programme for a long time."
B "**Neither have** I."
(= Ich auch nicht.)

Du verwendest [1]..............................., um einer positiven Aussage zuzustimmen.
Du verwendest [2]..............................., um einer negativen Aussage zuzustimmen.

MORE fun with Fido!

UNIT 18 Get active!

Vocabulary Sports

SbX

1 Write the numbers of the sports in each picture.

play:	go:		
1 football	**5** mountain climbing	**9** ice skating	**13** surfing
2 tennis	**6** cycling	**10** skateboarding	**14** windsurfing
3 basketball	**7** mountain biking	**11** swimming	**15** skiing
4 volleyball	**8** roller-skating	**12** snowboarding	**16** running

25 CD 3

2 Listen and check your answers.

Get talking Sports

3 **Ask and answer questions about some of the sports in 1.**

Do you like … ?
What's your favourite … team?
Do you play/go … ?
How often do you … ?
Do you like watching … on TV?
Who's your favourite sportsman/sportswoman?

26 CD 3 SbX

4 **Listen to the interviews with these two American teenagers and complete the profiles.**

This is 14-year-old Danni from California. Her favourite sport is surfing. She started surfing when she was [1] .... years old. She lives near the [2] .... in Santa Barbara. She goes surfing [3] .... a day.

This is 14-year-old Ricky from Colorado. His favourite sport is mountain climbing. He started climbing when he was [4] .... years old. He always goes climbing with his [5] .... They go about [6] .... times a month. They usually go climbing in the Rocky Mountains. They live [7] .... miles away from the Rocky Mountains National Park.

5 **Look at the questions below from the interviews. Which questions do you think are for:**

a) Danni? **b)** Ricky?

1 Have you ever won any competitions?
2 Have you ever got lost in the mountains?
3 Have you ever seen a shark?
4 Have you ever had an accident?
5 Have you ever climbed the Matterhorn?
6 Have you ever been to Australia?

27 CD 3

6 **Listen and check. Then listen again. Are their answers to the questions *yes* or *no*?**

WB p. 112

Get talking Asking questions with *Have you ever ... ?*

SbX

7 **Work in small groups. Ask and answer questions to find someone who has ...**

1 met a famous person.
2 won a competition.
3 appeared on television.
4 found some money.
5 lived in another country.
6 been to a pop concert.
7 fallen asleep in a lesson.
8 written a poem.

A Have you ever met a famous person?
B Yes, I have.
A Who?
B ...
A When was that?
B ...

28 CD 3 MP3

8 **Read and listen to the poem.**

The game

Eleven of us were on the field.
The other team looked scared.
"We're going to win," our trainer said.
"We're really well prepared."

Then Johnny kicked the ball to Paul
and Paul kicked it to Sue,
when Sue's mum shouted "Come home,
Sue, there's work for you to do."

Ten of us were on the field
and Helen tackled Eddie.
Then Mr Sutton arrived and said
"Triplets, your dinner's ready."

Seven of us were on the field.
The other team then scored.
And Tom and Helen said "We're off,
we're getting really bored."

Five of us were on the field,
when Roland hurt his knee.
He left. And Lisa went with him.
And then we were only three.

Three of us were on the field.
The score was twenty – nil.
"I've had enough. It's a waste of time."
And off the field went Phil.

Two of us were on the field
and we tried our very best.
But then Johnny turned to me and said
"I'm off, I need a rest."

So there I was all on my own,
a goalie without a team.
Then Dad called out "Wake up! You're late."
Thank God – it was just a dream.

CYBER HOMEWORK 35

9 **Read the text and complete the sentences.**

Extreme sports profile

ACTION MAN

Who is he?
Felix Baumgartner, from Austria.

What does he do?
Base jumping, free fall, free-flying.

Tell me more.
Base jumping is an extreme type of parachuting. People who do it jump from low heights (buildings, radio masts, bridges and mountains, for example) and only open their parachute at the last moment.

Where has he jumped from?
He's jumped from the statue of Christ in Rio de Janeiro, from the Petronas Towers in Kuala Lumpur and the Taipei 101 Tower (the tallest buildings in the world at the time). He's also jumped from the bridge in Panama that connects North and South America. (He spent some nights in prison for that.)

In December 2004 he jumped from a helicopter in Rio de Janeiro. He opened his parachute only 50 metres before he hit the beach in Copacabana. It was a world record.

What is he most famous for?
When he crossed the English Channel on July 31st, 2003, he jumped from a plane at 9,000 metres. He only had a small parachute and a carbon wing on his back. He flew 35 kilometres in 14 minutes from the English coast to the French coast.

What do the papers call him?
Birdman Baumgartner, Fearless Felix.

What does he say about his sport?
"I love it. I enjoy the total freedom of free-flying. And I like the challenge. Sometimes it's hard work. For the English Channel flight, I needed three years to prepare, but it was worth it."

1 Felix Baumgartner is from ....
2 His sports are ....
3 He's jumped from many ....
4 For his jump in Panama, he ....
5 In 2004 he jumped ....
6 He is most famous for ....
7 The free flight was from .... to ...., and it lasted ....
8 He really loves ....

WB p. 113

10 **Read the text and match the sentence halves.**

Extreme sports profile

ACTION WOMAN

Who is she?
Emma Sanderson, from England.

What does she do?
She's a yachtswoman.

Tell me more.
She sails a yacht, in team races or alone.

What competitions has she won?
She won the Round Britain and Ireland Race in 2000 at the age of 25 and also the Europe 1 New Man Star from Plymouth to Rhode Island, USA.

What is she most famous for?
She won the 'Around Alone' race in 2002/03. She was the youngest woman and first British person to complete the 29,000 mile solo around-the-world yacht race. She was at sea for over 135 days. She had to face a hurricane, pirates and the extreme weather of the Southern Ocean – and, of course, she was alone at sea for four and a half months.

What does she say about her sport?
"I love the challenge. I don't really like being alone for a long time - I'm a people person. But I really wanted to be in the 'Around Alone' race. I'm also in a Global Education Programme and now I can tell kids about my sailing. I really enjoy that."

1	Emma Sanderson is an	☐	complete the 29,000 mile solo race.
2	She sails in	☐	about her sailing.
3	She won many team races,	☐	team races or alone.
4	She was the youngest woman to	☐	English yachtswoman.
5	She doesn't like being	☐	but she's really famous for the 'Around Alone' race.
6	Now she enjoys telling kids	☐	alone for such a long time, but she loves the challenge.

Sounds right /ɔː/ /əʊ/

29 CD 3

11 **Which is the odd one out? Listen and check.**

1	a) more	b) board	c) coat
2	a) door	b) go	c) slow
3	a) four	b) know	c) saw
4	a) sport	b) bought	c) toe

WB p. 114

Writing *for your Portfolio*

12 **Write a text about your favourite sport.**

● Text 1

My favourite sport is skiing. I love it. In the winter I go skiing every weekend because I live in the mountains. I like watching it on TV, too. It's really exciting. My favourite skiers are all from Austria. They're really good.

■ Text 2

I love volleyball. I love playing it and I love watching it on TV too. There are some great teams like Brazil and Italy. I like playing it because it's a fantastic team sport. It's also a brilliant way to make friends. I play in the school team. We're very good. Last year we won 18 out of 20 games. Once I broke my arm playing volleyball. I couldn't play for three months. My dream is to play professional volleyball.

SbX

Grammar Present perfect with *ever* and *never*

Wenn du fragen willst, ob jemand **irgendwann** in der Vergangenheit etwas getan oder erlebt hat, dann verwendest du meist das *present perfect*.
Du verwendest es auch um ausdrücken, dass du etwas nie getan oder erlebt hast.
Häufig verwendest du in diesen Situationen die Wörter *ever* und *never*.

Have you **ever** seen a shark?
Have you **ever** won a competition?

I've **never** had an accident.
I've **never** got lost in the mountains.

UNIT 19 Light rain in the north

1 **Look at the map and read the text. Change the Fahrenheit temperatures into Celsius. Use this scale to help you.**

F	0	10	20	30	40	50	60	70	80	90	100
C	-18	-12	-7	-1	4	10	16	21	27	32	38

Note:

The formula is:
$C = (F - 32) : 1{,}8$

The weather today

The good weather continues. Early morning clouds give way to lots of sunshine. Nicely cool and dry at the coast with lower temperatures in the North. Very hot in the South with temperatures in the 100s Fahrenheit.

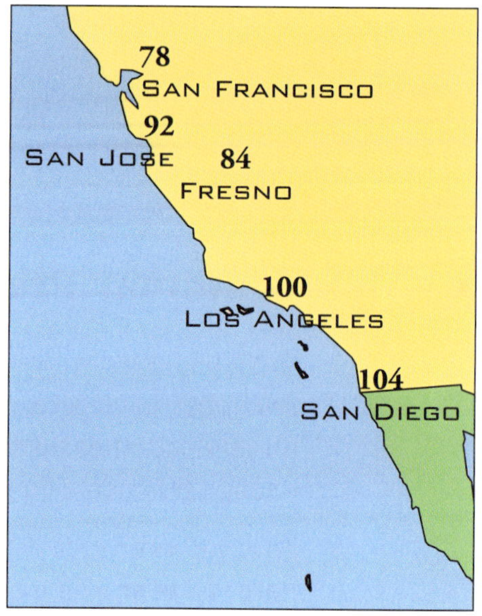

Vocabulary Weather

30 CD 3 SbX

2 **Listen and number. Then test your partner.**

1 hot **2** cold **3** clouds **4** thunderstorm **5** snow **6** fog **7** rain **8** sunny **9** windy

31
CD 3

3 Listen to the weather forecast.
Then read it and draw the missing symbol on the maps.

Note:
° = degrees

Today:
Sunny, some clouds north of Leicester. Thick fog in the Stoke area will clear up later. Temperatures between 3°C and 12°C. Winds 10-20 mph.

Outlook for tomorrow:
Light rain in the Stoke area. Sunny in the Leicester area. More rain in the Malverns and thunderstorms coming from the north in the evening. Strong winds. Temperatures between 8°C and 15°C.

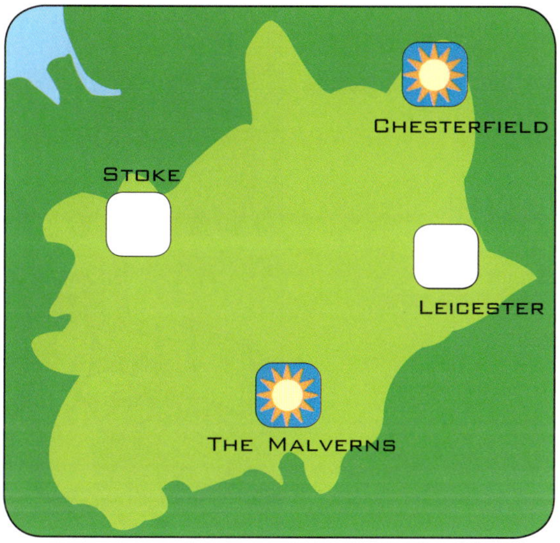

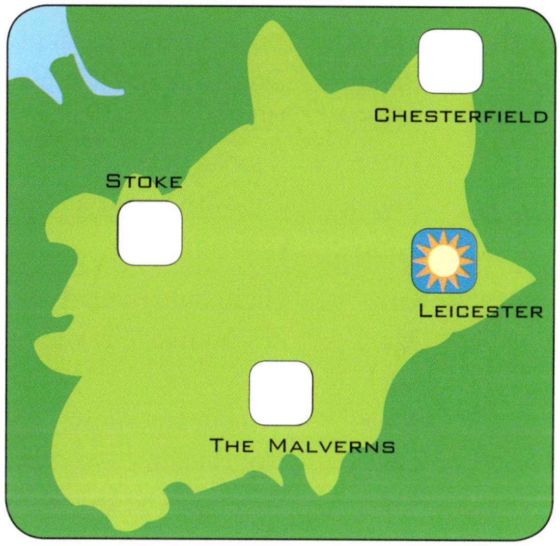

32
CD 3
SbX

4 Look at the maps of the UK. Listen to the weather forecasts and draw the symbols.

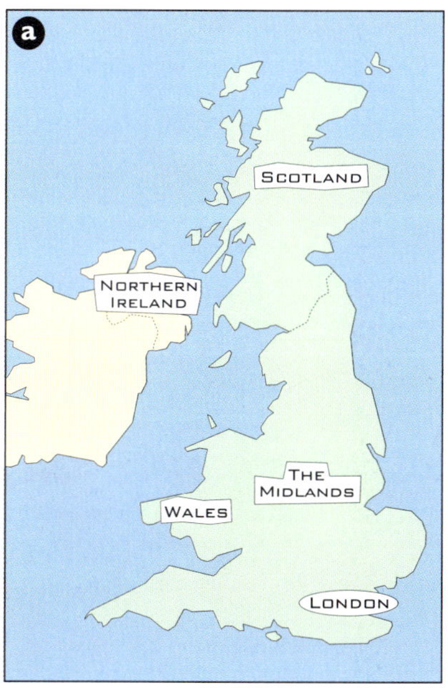

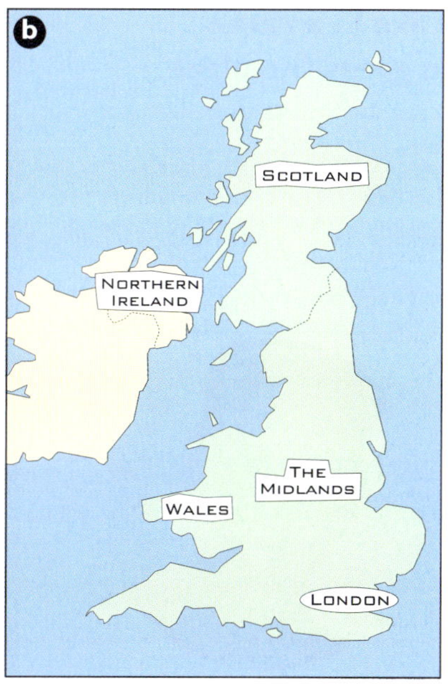

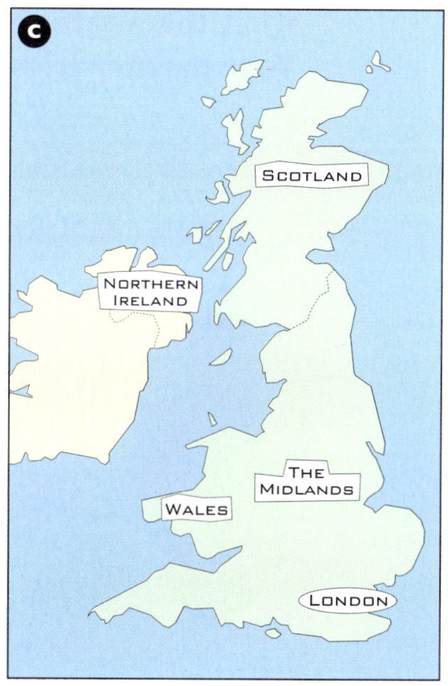

WB p. 118   CYBER HOMEWORK 37

33 CD 3 MP3

5 Read and listen to the dialogues. Then act them out.

Dialogue 1

Monica Hi, Robert, I'm taking the next train to London. I'll be at your place at about six.
Robert Great. I'll have dinner ready.
Monica What's the weather like in London?
Robert Fine. There might be some rain in the evening. Don't forget your umbrella.
Monica I won't.

Dialogue 2

Maria Where are you going?
Peter Don't worry. I'll be back. I'm getting my raincoat.
Maria Why?
Peter It looks like rain.
Maria You won't need it. We're getting a taxi.

Dialogue 3

Girl Highland Hotel, Aviemore. Can I help you?
Man Yes, I'd like to ask about a skiing holiday.
Girl Yes?
Man Is there any snow?
Girl Not yet, sir.
Man Will there be any snow next week?
Girl They say there will be, sir – but I can't promise anything.

Get talking Asking about the weather

6 Work in pairs. Look at the map and say what the weather is like in an area. Your partner tries to guess the place.

A There is thick fog and the temperature is 10°C.

B You're in London.

Time for a sketch

34 CD 3 MP3 SbX

7 **Listen and read. Then act out the sketch.**

"And the weather for tomorrow … "

Dad OK, have we finished packing? Has everybody got their swimming trunks and bathing suits?

Jane Yes, Dad. Do I need a sweater?

Dad I don't think so. It won't be very cold in the evenings. *(Turns to Jamie.)* Jamie, turn off the TV. We're leaving in a few minutes.

Jamie Just a second, Dad. The weather report is coming on. Hey Dad, listen to this.

(He turns up the volume.)

Weatherman

… In the south of England showers will be quite heavy and the sun won't come out for another few days. Temperatures will drop to 10° Celsius during the night and only go up to 17° Celsius during the day. There might also be a few thunderstorms. The weather situation will only get better after the weekend – and that's all from us for today.

Mum Turn it down, Jamie. Come here, and help with the unpacking.

Jane Oh, Mum. Why do we have to unpack?

Dad Your mum's right. We have to take out all the swimming things and put in a few sweaters. Come on, kids, it's a long way to the coast.

(They start unpacking.)

Jane What about my sweater? Will I need it?

Mum Yes, of course. And the raincoat too.

(15 minutes later.)

Dad Right. Have we got everything? And Jamie!!! Turn off the TV!

Jamie But Dad …

Dad Turn it off!

Jamie Look, the weatherman is on again.

Mum Let's hear what he's got to say.

(Jamie turns up the volume.)

Weatherman

… have to apologise. I'm very sorry, but I gave you last week's weather report. I'm very sorry. Now here's the correct weather report for the next few days. Sunshine wherever we look, with temperatures going up to 25 to 30° Celsius. Some light cloud in the evenings, but there's nothing to worry about.

Dad OK! Let's start again!

★ **8** **Read the two texts and convert the numbers from Fahrenheit to Centigrade, feet to metres and inches to centimetres.**

Note:
O°F = -18°C
1 ft (foot) = 30,48 centimetres
1 inch = 2,54 centimetres

The hottest place in the USA

Death Valley is generally sunny, dry and clear throughout the year. The winters are mild, but summers are very hot and dry. In fact, Death Valley is one of the hottest places on earth. The highest temperature ever recorded in the USA was 134°F on July 10th, 1913. Summer high temperatures are usually around 120°F. The average rainfall each year is two inches.
Death Valley has the lowest point in the western world – 282 feet below sea level near Badwater – as well as many high mountains such as Telescope Peak at over 11,000 feet.

The wettest place in England

The wettest place in England is in the Lake District. It is a small village called Seatoller. Seatoller is the starting point for some great walks. But bring good clothes against the rain. The average rainfall each year is 120 inches. Some people say there is even more rainfall in Seathwaite (one mile away): 130 inches.
Seatoller doesn't have more rainy days than other places – but when it rains, it rains more.

Writing *for your Portfolio*

9 **Write a holiday postcard to a friend and also tell him/her about the weather.**

● **Text 1**

Dear Sophie,
It's raining and raining and raining. My clothes are wet and they won't dry. The TV doesn't work. Dad says "Read a good book," but I've already read three (!!!) books. Another three days to go! (☹)
Love,
Gemma

■ **Text 2**

Dear Ken,
Everything's great. The food, the hotel, the weather. We've had sunshine all week long, and they say there won't be any rain for another two weeks. Pity we have to leave at the end of next week. I've got a great tan! And we've been to the beach every day.
The surf is great, too. Maybe I'll try windsurfing, too.
See you!
Silvia

▶ WB p. 119

Sounds right /l/

35 CD 3

10 **Listen. Number the sentences as you hear them.**

☐ I do it every day.	☐ They see us on Fridays.
☐ I'll speak English to her.	☐ We'll tell you a joke.
☐ We tell jokes a lot.	☐ They'll see us on Friday.
☐ I speak English quite well.	☐ I'll do it my way.

SbX

Grammar *Will* - future

Mit Hilfe der *will-future* drückst du Erwartungen, Hoffnungen und Vermutungen für die Zukunft aus.

We **will meet** again. (We**'ll meet** again.)

I **will not go** away for a very long time. (I **won't go** away for a very long time.)

Du verwendest die *will-future* auch dann, wenn du etwas vorhersagen willst:

Some heavy rain **will come** in from Northern Scotland.

The south of England **will have** quite a lot of fog near the coast.

The sun **won't come** out for another few days.

Du verwendest die *will-future* auch dann, wenn du dich spontan zu entschließt oder spontan versprichst, etwas zu tun.

Maybe **I'll try** sailing, too.

I'll help you with your homework tonight.

Complete with *'ll / will / won't*.

Bildung: Person + [1]...................... *(not)* + *base form* des Verbs

Kurzformen: I will = I [2]...................... I will not = I [3]...................... .

1 How much do you remember about your English book? Do the quiz and find out.

The MORE QUIZ!

1 In Unit 1 Sara told a holiday story about this animal. What is it?

a The yellow back octopus
b The blue ring octopus
c The blue spot octopus

2 What did Charles (the hypnotist) say to wake Roger up in Unit 2?

a Pronto!
b Hello!
c Wake up!

3 In Unit 3 Mrs Smith worked in a museum. What was her job?

a director
b cleaner
c sculptor

4 This boy disappeared in Unit 4. What was his name?

a Larry
b George
c Jim

5 In Unit 5 you met this fantastic animal from Atlantis. What was it called?

a a Snapkle
b a Ruckle
c a Hipcop

6 In Unit 6 Danielle got lost in an English town. Where was she from?

a France
b Spain
c Italy

7 What did Gillie find on the geo caching treasure hunt adventure in Unit 7?

a an old boot
b a diamond
c old coins

WB p. 123

8 Why was William so worried in Unit 8?

a He had a German test.
b He had a driving test.
c He had no money.

9 In Unit 9 we learnt that Fido has a friend. When does he usually see him?

a in the morning
b in the afternoon
c in the evening

10 What was the name of the best restaurant in town in Unit 10?

a Mario's
b Dave and Jill's
c Johnny's

11 This is Ra, an Egyptian god from Unit 11. What was he the god of?

a the moon
b the stars
c the sun

12 In Unit 12 you met Mr and Mrs Albina. How many children do they have?

a 13
b 33
c 53

13 Here's the teacher ghost from Unit 13. Where did he get stuck?

a in the wall
b in the toilet
c in the door

14 In Unit 14 you read about this house. What is unusual about it?

a It's really big.
b It's made of tyres.
c It's got no windows.

15 In Unit 15 Mr Wilkins wanted a pill. What colour was it?

a pink
b blue
c yellow

16 In Unit 17, Wallace the dog talked to a friend. What was the friend's name?

a Dover
b Rover
c Randolph

36 CD 3

2 Listen and check your answers. Score one point for every answer you get right. Who's got the best memory in the class?

WB p. 124 CYBER HOMEWORK 39

SbX

3 Read the diary of Marcus White. What day of the week do these things happen?

1. Marcus wants a new best friend.
2. Marcus runs a race.
3. Marcus gets told off in the school assembly.
4. Marcus makes a list.
5. Marcus is late for school.
6. Marcus gets his school results.

Sunday

Fantastic. Great. Wonderful. Finally – it's here!
The last week of school for two months.
Two months of holiday!
Oh, what a happy week!
Things to do for my holidays
- Paint my bedroom black.
- Do karate lessons.
- Beat my dad at chess.
- Read all the Lemony Snicket books – again!
- Get fit!
- Build a new go-kart with Sam (my best friend this week)

Spend time with Jenny – this might be difficult because I've never spoken to her in my life.
I'll definitely need a plan for this.

Monday

School was a bit boring.
I got my test results. 'C' for everything.
'C' isn't so bad. It's better than 'D'.
I explained this to dad. He didn't really understand. I don't think he's very happy at the moment.
I think he's got problems at work.
I forgot to ask Jenny for her phone number.
I must do this tomorrow.
Four days to go!

Tuesday

I had a big argument with my dad at breakfast today. He says I can't paint my bedroom black.
It's got to be blue. Blue! My dad doesn't understand teenagers. I'm not going to speak to him for a week.
School was better. We played games all day. I think our teachers are very tired.
There was one bad thing. Sam had some news for me – Jenny is going to live in London.
She's not going to be at our school next term.
"What!?" I screamed.
Then Sam said it was a joke.
I think I need a new best friend.

Wednesday

Another bad breakfast. I asked my dad for £10 to buy some wood for my go-kart. Dad said "Have you forgotten? You're not speaking to me." He's so smart. So I asked mum because I'm still speaking to her. She said "Ask your dad." Parents are complicated.
It was Sports Day at school today. I was in the 2,000 metres – five times around the running track! I got a new school record – the slowest time in the history of Sports Day. It was the last race of the day. When I finished, nobody was there. That was a shame because I wanted to ask Jenny for her phone number. I must do this tomorrow.

Thursday

I got up half an hour late today because I didn't want to see dad at breakfast. The plan worked. I didn't see him. The only problem was I was half an hour late for school.
My teacher wasn't happy.
We had the school play this afternoon.
I don't really remember what the story was about. But Jenny was in it. She was great. After the play everybody wanted to talk to her. I couldn't ask her for her phone number. There were too many people. I'm going to be in the school play next year.

Friday

Today we had the final assembly with Mr Hill, the headmaster. He read out all the names of the best students. The best students at Maths, the best students at Science, at Sport, at French, etc. Then he shouted out my name – not because I'm best at anything (unfortunately) but because I was talking to my friend. Everyone looked at me. Jenny looked at me. I think she smiled. I went red. I didn't ask Jenny for her phone number but I've got a new plan. I'm going to talk to Jenny next term. I'll be thirteen then. I read in a book that talking to girls is easier when you're thirteen!

WB p. 125

A Song 4 U *We're on holiday*

37/38 CD 3 MP3 SbX

4 **Listen and sing.**

When the school bell rings
at a quarter to four
and we pack up our things
and we walk out that door

And we say goodbye
to teachers and friends,
it's the end of July
and the term's at an end.

We can do anything.
We can go anywhere.
No more lessons for a long, long time.
We're on holiday, on holiday,
on holiday. We feel fine!

Have you got any plans,
what to do with your time?
Let's go to the beach
if the weather's fine.

Are you going away
to France or to Spain?
Or are you going to stay
at home and play?

We can do …

If you're feeling bored,
just give me a call.
We can all meet up
at the shopping mall.

We can buy a new film
on DVD and then go home
and watch TV.

We can do …

More fun with Fido!

5 **How well do you remember Fido?**
Write the numbers of the sentences in the speech bubbles.

1 I'm the fattest dog in the world.
2 I'm happy the holidays are over.
3 Here's firefighter Fido. Make way!
4 That's the curse of the mummy!
5 My compliments to the chef.
6 Fido has returned!!
7 Up, and down!
8 That's not what I wanted.
9 Now, what did I do wrong.
10 You don't have to use a GPS with a nose like mine.

Kids in NYC 4

The missing cat

Note:

cell phone = American English
mobile (phone) = British English

Before you watch

1 Write the words under the pictures.

market
cell phone
reward

1.................. 2.................. 3..................

2 In what order do you think these pictures come in the DVD? Write 1–4 in the boxes.

A

B

C
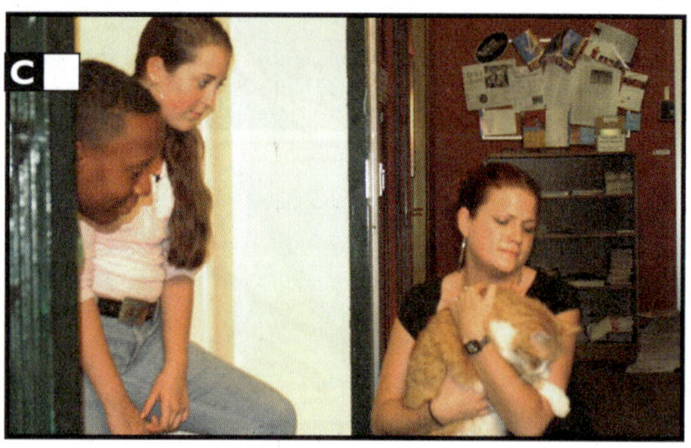

D

3 In pairs, invent a story that goes with the pictures in 2.

Watch the story

4 Check your answers to 2.

5 Complete the sentences.

1 Steve and Jenny see ....
2 They want to ....
3 First they want to look ....and ....
4 Then Jenny has an idea. She wants to look for the cat ....
5 She thinks they might find the cat there because ....

6 Complete the dialogue.

think
look
see
get
check

Jenny [1].................... that cat? Doesn't it [2].................... like Tiger?
Steve No. I don't [3].................... so. But look. There behind that box.
Let's [4].................... with the picture.
Jenny Yeah, it looks a bit like Tiger. [5].................... him.
Steve Here kitty, kitty. Here kitty. Got you, Tiger.

7 Circle T (*True*) or F (*False*).

1	Jenny and Steve find Tiger at the fish market.	T / F
2	They find Tiger under a car.	T / F
3	They put Tiger in a bag.	T / F
4	The man at the fish market has a cat and a dog.	T / F
5	Jenny and Steve give Tiger to the man.	T / F
6	The woman gives Jenny and Steve a $20 reward.	T / F

Everyday English

8 Complete the dialogues.

I don't get it.
Got you,
What for?
Right here.

Progress Check Units 16–20

Listening

39 CD 3

Listen to the weather forecasts. Complete the forecasts with the words from the box. There are five words that you will not use.

sun	snow	clouds	dry	sunny spells
mild	thunderstorms	rain	hot	warm

The weather for the UK for Saturday

More 1 .... along the east coast and maybe 2.. in the afternoon. England and Wales: 3.. and mild.

The weather for Ireland for Saturday

Cloudy with 4.. in the morning. Rain in the north and east in the afternoon. The south will be dry and 5.. Temperatures will be between 19°C and 22°C.

☐ 5

Reading

Read the text. Circle T *(True)* or F *(False)*.

The coldest places in the universe

Some of the coldest temperatures anywhere are in outer space. One example is the Boomerang Nebula. It is 5,000 light-years from Earth. The temperature there is about -170°C all the time.

An even colder spot is Pluto. Scientists believe the average temperature there is about -220°C.
Earth is 92 million miles away from the sun, and Jupiter is five times further away than that. Earth gets 6 times as much heat as Jupiter and 30 times as much heat as Pluto.

The coldest temperatures on earth are mild! Canada's coldest place, for example, is Eureka, on Ellesmere Island. The average temperature throughout the year is -19.9°C, but in February, usually the coldest month, the average temperature is -38.4°C. In February 1979, people recorded the lowest average temperature ever in Canada: -47.9°C. For 18 days, the thermometer stayed below -45°C. On February 15, the station recorded the lowest temperature of all. It was -55.3°C.

1 The Boomerang Nebula has temperatures around -5,000°C.	T / F
2 Earth is further away from the sun than Jupiter.	T / F
3 Jupiter gets more heat from the sun than Pluto.	T / F
4 The coldest place in the universe is Eureka, on Ellesmere Island in Canada.	T / F
5 In 1979 the temperature in Eureka was colder than -50°C.	T / F

☐ 5

Grammar

Circle the correct answer.

1 I'm not hungry. I've *already / yet* eaten.
2 Susan's not here any more. I think *she's gone / she goes* home.
3 *Do you / Have you* done your homework?
4 **A** I love lemon ice cream.
B *So have I. / So do I.*
5 **A** I haven't read this book.
B *Neither have I. / Neither do I.*
6 **A** Do you know Tina's brother Ron?
B No, I've *ever / never* met him.
7 **A** Have you *ever / never* won any prize?
B No, never.
8 Bye, bye, Tom. *We meet / We'll meet* again.
9 Tomorrow some heavy rain *will fall / fall.*
10 The weather's nice now, but *there'll be / there are* some light showers later.

☐ **10**

Vocabulary

Complete the sentences about keeping a pet.

1 Don't .... a cat more often than twice a day. Cats shouldn't eat too much!
2 Ted has a hamster. He .... its cage once a week.
3 Jim has got a dog. He .... him in the park.
4 If your cat has long hair, you must .... it once a week.
5 Tom's cat was ill a week ago. So Tom took her to the ....

☐ **5**

Dialogue

Tick the best answers.

1 What's the weather like?
☐ A I don't like it really.
☐ B There might be some really.
☐ C I like it when it's cool.

2 Have you ever seen a snake?
☐ A I've never been there.
☐ B Yes, I have.
☐ C Neither have I.

3 How often do you go running?
☐ A I like cycling.
☐ B I've never run a marathon.
☐ C Four times a week.

4 I like walking my dog.
☐ A No, I'm not.
☐ B I ask them round.
☐ C So do I.

5 What do you like about this video game?
☐ A The graphics are awesome.
☐ B I played it until midnight.
☐ C I've already logged in.

☐ **5**

How did you do?

	☺	😐	☹
Listening	4-5	2-3	0-1
Reading	4-5	2-3	0-1
Grammar	7-10	4-6	0-3
Vocabulary	4-5	2-3	0-1
Dialogue	4-5	2-3	0-1
Total	21-30	11-20	0-10

CLIL

A short history of Australia

KEY WORDS

land	nation	Member of Parliament
discovery	vote	colony
gold	aborigines	drive (someone) from their land.

40 CD 3

1 Complete the time line. Then listen and check.

South Australia: women over 21 can vote.
Australia becomes a British colony.
The discovery of gold.
Aborigines can vote.

40,000BC	The Aborigines are already in Australia.
2000BC	The dingo is the first 'pet' to come to Australia.
1770	Captain Cook lands on the east coast of Australia.
1778	....
1851	.... Many people come to Australia and drive the Aborigines from their land.
1860	The explorer John Stuart visits Central Australia.
1894	....
1901	Australia becomes a nation.
1962	....
1971	Neville Bonner is the first Aboriginal to become a Member of Parliament.
2000	The Sydney Olympics.

2a **Read the text.**

Women and Australian History

Australia was one of the first countries in the world to give women the right to vote. In 1894, women in South Australia could vote for the first time, but not Aborigines or women under the age of 21. Australia was still a British colony, but women in Britain could not vote. Women in Britain waited until 1918, and then only women over the age of 30 could vote.

Women in other states of Australia voted for the first time in 1903 but they could not stand for election until the end of World War One. Today, there are 37 women in the Australian Parliament's House of Representatives.

2b **Now answer these questions about your country.**

1 Can women vote in your country?
2 How old must you be to vote?
3 When did men win the right to vote?
4 When did women win the right to vote?

Mini Project The history of Australian place names

3 Some towns and cities in Australia have the same names as towns/cities in Britain - the British, of course, took the names there.

Here are the names of ten towns/cities in Australia:

Sydney Mackay Newcastle Brisbane Townsville Melbourne Adelaide Canberra Perth Cairns

i) Copy the map of Australia and put the towns/cities in the correct place on it. Use an atlas or the Internet to help you.

ii) Find out (use your library or the Internet) which two of these are named after towns/cities in Britain.

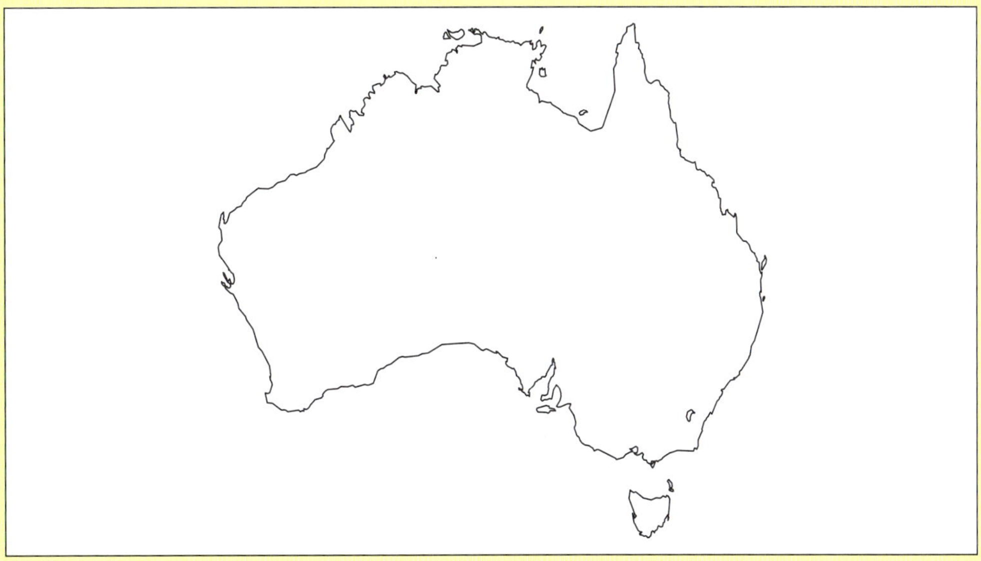

CLIL

Geographical features of South America

KEY WORDS

field	tribe	deep	volcano	waterfall
wool	rainforest	wide	desert	lake

41 CD 3

1 The South America Quiz. Tick the correct answer. Then listen and check.

1 How many people live in South America?
a) about 400 million ☐ b) about 200 million ☐
c) about 100 million ☐ d) about 50 million ☐

2 What are the two main languages of South America?
a) Spanish and French ☐ b) Spanish and Portuguese ☐
c) French and Portuguese ☐ d) English and Spanish ☐

3 Which is the biggest country?
a) Venezuela ☐ b) Ecuador ☐ c) Chile ☐ d) Brazil ☐

4 Which four countries are not in South America?
a) Argentina ☐ b) Bolivia ☐ c) Chile ☐ d) Sweden ☐
e) Brazil ☐ f) Vietnam ☐ g) Peru ☐ h) Uruguay ☐
i) Iran ☐ j) Colombia ☐ k) Canada ☐ l) Venezuela ☐

2 Read the texts and match the geographical features with the letters on the map.

1 River ☐

The Amazon is a very big river. It is more than 6,400 kilometres long. It flows through Colombia, Peru, Bolivia and Brazil. There is more water in this river than any other river in the world.

2 Lake ☐

Lake Titicaca is on the border between Bolivia and Peru. It is 3,810 metres above sea level. It is also a deep lake, in places about 180 metres deep. This lake is almost a small sea. It is more than 190 kilometres long and about 80 kilometres wide. There are also 41 islands in the lake.

3 Waterfall ☐

The Angel Falls in Venezuela are nearly 1,000 metres high. In very hot weather the water can evaporate before it reaches the bottom.

4 Desert ☐

The Atacama desert in Chile is about 1,000 kilometres long. It is also 15 million years old. It is very dry: on average there is 1mm of rain per year.

5 Rainforest ☐

The Amazon rainforest covers a billion acres including the countries Brazil, Venezuela, Colombia, Ecuador and Peru. It produces about 20% of the planet's oxygen. More than 50% of the world's species of plants, insects and animals live in the Amazon Rainforest.

3 **Read the text and then complete the fact file about Brazil.**

FACT FILE

Brazil is the largest country in South America. Its capital city is Brasilia. About 182.8 million people live in Brazil and the official language is Portuguese. Some important exports from Brazil are oranges and coffee. The most important geographical features of Brazil are the Amazon River and the Amazon Rainforest. One major problem in Brazil is the destruction of the rainforest. Many animals and plants are disappearing as a result. Many tribes that lived in the rainforest don't exist any more.

Name: Brazil

Capital: ....

Population: ....

Official Language: ....

Exports: ....

Major geographical features: Amazon River, ...

Problems: destruction of the rainforest ....

Mini Project A country in South America

4 **Make a poster about a country in South America. On the poster:**

- put a map with the capital city and 1 or 2 more cities
- put pictures of any important mountains / rivers / lakes / etc.
- put pictures of any animals that are found in the country
- write some sentences with the information you found

Use books or the Internet to find the information.

5 **Write a fact file about your country. Use the Internet or a library to help you.**

CLIL

Robots

KEY WORDS

robot	a machine	factory
intelligent machine	work automatically	put cars together
programme	industrial robots	produce

1 What is a robot?

All robots are intelligent machines. They are made up of two elements:

1 They have got a body.

2 When you programme them, they work automatically.

2 Read the text.

ROBOT FACTS

Most robots today are industrial robots. Humans use them to make work easier and quicker. You often see them in car factories where they put the cars together. They are useful for this kind of work as it is ' dull, dirty and dangerous' - DDD. Robots are often used for DDD jobs and where a specific action needs to be repeated. It is very difficult for humans to do this.

There are many different types of robots. Some robots travel through space, work on the bottom of the ocean, or go inside volcanoes. These are places that are very dangerous for people, or impossible for people to go to.

Robots are everywhere. Most people don't know that robots help us every day and in many different ways. In most houses there are robots. For example, in some houses today there is a washing machine in the kitchen. Washing machines are robots. People can programme them and then they wash clothes automatically.

Some scientists make robots for fun: for example, the dogs in this photo.

Japan produces the most robots. Every year in the capital, Tokyo, there is a robot exhibition called Robodex. It is the largest robot exhibition in the world.

Learn MORE through English

3 **Which of these are robots? Discuss in class.**

traffic light

DVD recorder

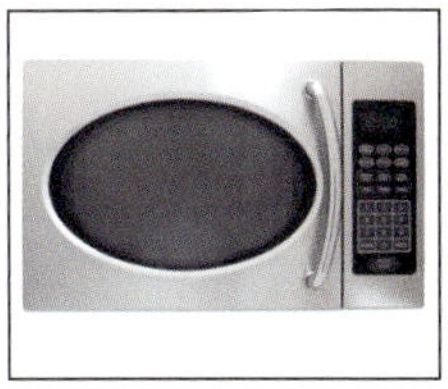

microwave

bicycle

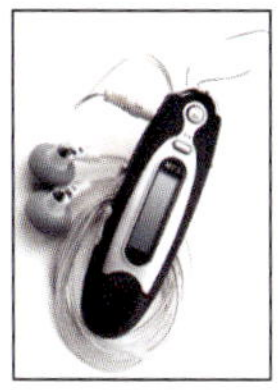

MP3

car

pen

alarm clock

torch

dishwasher

A dishwasher is a robot. We can programme it and it works automatically.

A torch is not a robot. We cannot programme it to work automatically.

Mini Project

4 **Make a note of the machines you use during a day. Look up the English names of the machines in a dictionary. Decide if they are robots. Write a diary for your day.**

These are the machines I used during the day:

Date	Time	Object	Is it a robot?
23rd May	*7.00 a.m.*	*alarm clock*	*Yes*
	7.50 a.m.	*toaster*	*Not sure!*
	8.30 a.m.	*bus*	....
	8.50 a.m.	*traffic lights*	....
	9.00 a.m.	*school bell*	....
	1.00 p.m.	*CD player*	....
	2.30 p.m.	*computer*	....
	5.30 p.m.	*automatic doors at supermarket*	....
	7.30 p.m.	....	....

5 **Ask and answer questions about the results.**

Did you use … in the morning? / on the way to school? / at school? / … ?
Do you think a … is a robot?
How many robots did you use in the morning? / … / all day?

The feeling of happiness

KEY WORDS

happiness	hunt for food	produce chemicals	health
feeling	motivate	alarm	

1 Match the pictures below with some of the key words.

Where does HAPPINESS come from?

Happiness is the most wonderful feeling in the world. In fact, most people would like to be happy all the time. Where does happiness come from? And why is it so difficult to be happy? Read these texts and find out.

1 Thousands of years ago life was very difficult and dangerous. There were lots of wild animals: bears, mammoths, tigers and wolves. People had to hunt these animals for food. That was dangerous, and not a lot of fun.

2 To motivate people to go hunting the brain invented a trick: the feeling of happiness. When people hunted an animal and had something good to eat, their brain produced two chemicals: serotonin and endorphin. These chemicals made people feel happy. The brain also produced these chemicals when someone was the winner in a fight or when people met their friends.

3 Today, we don't hunt wild animals. But our brain still produces the same chemicals. For example, when we eat our favourite food, when we meet our friends, when we listen to our favourite music, when we do well at school or when we play a sport and our team wins.

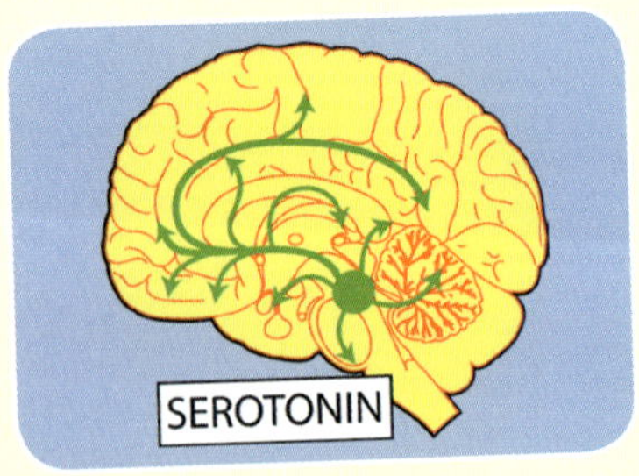

The bad news: we can't be happy all the time!

4 Let's look back thousands of years again. Imagine people were sitting around a fire, eating a nice piece of tiger steak. Suddenly they heard something from behind a bush. Their brain produced another chemical, dopamine. Alarm! And their feeling of happiness was gone.

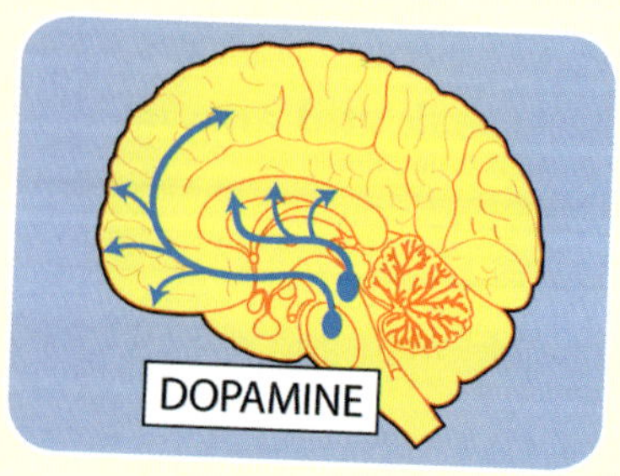

The good news: we can train our brain to be happy!

5 Experts say you can train your brain to be happy. It is often small things that make us unhappy. It can help to try and think of positive things more often. Another good idea is to keep a happiness diary. Write three positive things in it every day. And before you fall asleep, think about what was good for you during the day.

Mini Project Happiness

2 **Keep a happiness diary for a week. Then make a chart of your week.**

10 = extremely happy / 0 = not happy

My happiness log **Date: ....**

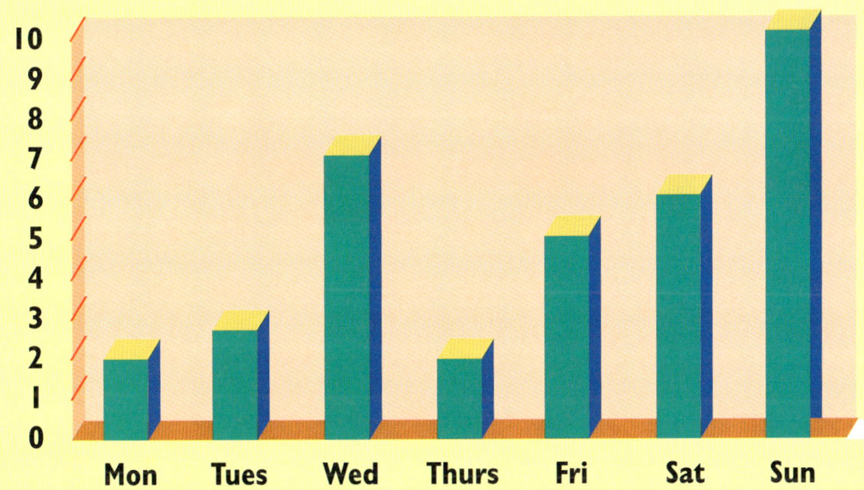

Last week was quite good. I did something nice every day. On Monday I watched an interesting DVD about wildlife in Africa with my mum. On Tuesday my friends and I had a lot of fun at school. Thursday was not so good – lots of Maths homework! On Friday I did well in an English test. ;-)) On Saturday my sister and I went to see our grandmother. We went for a walk with her dog. Sunday was fantastic. It was my birthday!

CLiL

Famous modern authors for young people

KEY WORDS

famous author	sell books	publish a book
journalist	popular book	translation
win prizes	publisher	invent a story / novel

1 Read the fact files about three famous authors for young people.

FACT FILE

Name: Jacqueline Wilson
Born: 1945, Bath, England.
Other jobs before writing: Journalist
Wrote first novel: 1954 (aged nine)
Famous novels: *Double Act, Vicky Angel, Girls in Love, Tracy Beaker, Kiss.*
Interesting fact: She has more than 15,000 books in her house!

FACT FILE

Name: Eoin Colfer
Born: 1965, Wexford, Ireland.
Other jobs before writing: Primary school teacher.
Wrote first novel: 1999
Famous novels: *Benny and Omar*, the *Artemis Fowl* series.
Interesting fact: He has worked in Saudi Arabia, Tunisia and Italy.

FACT FILE

Name: Jerry Spinelli
Born: 1941, Pennsylvania, USA
Other jobs before writing: Editor
Wrote first novel: 1982
Famous novels: *Maniac Magee, Stargirl, Loser* and *Eggs.*
Interesting fact: He wanted to be a baseball player. When he was 16, he wrote a poem about a football game. The local newspaper published it!

Learn MORE through English

2 **Read the summaries of three novels. Which book would you like to read?**

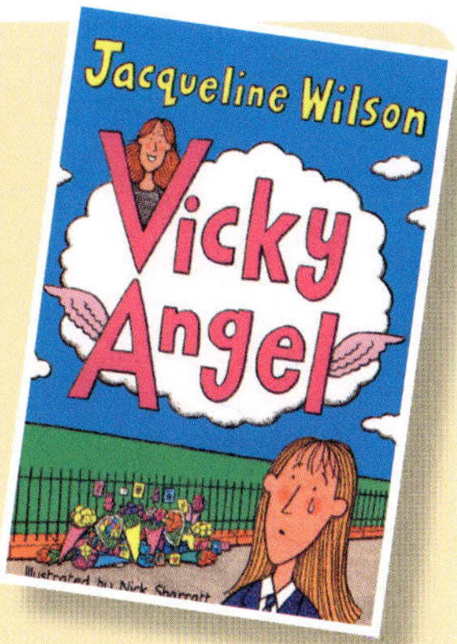

Vicky Angel by Jacqueline Wilson
Jade and Vicky have been best friends since kindergarten. One day the two girls argue. The same day Vicky gets run over by a car. Jade cannot forget Vicky. She tries to make new friends. But one day Vicky appears again as a ghost. Jade is happy but other people see that she is talking to herself and they think she is crazy. Jade goes and sees a psychologist who helps her to find out who she really is.

Maniac Magee by Jerry Spinelli
Jeffrey 'Maniac' Magee is a young white boy whose parents die in an accident. Jeffrey starts to live with his aunt and uncle, but he soon runs away from home and lives for some time in a zoo. Then a black family takes him in. Jeffrey soon finds out that there is a problem. In the town there are black people who live in the East End and white people who live in the West End. Jeffrey doesn't understand why the blacks and whites do not like one another. He travels throughout the town and tries to change how the people think.

Artemis Fowl by Eoin Colfer
Artemis Fowl is twelve years old. The Fowls are an old Irish family. Artemis wants to get rich. He finds out that fairies and elves exist and that they have magical books. He plans to get one. He hopes that the book will show him how to get the gold treasure of the fairies. With the help of his butler he tricks an old fairy woman. She lends him her magical book but only for thirty minutes. Artemis scans it with a digital camera and emails it to his computer. He tries to find out about the treasure of the fairies. But he needs help so he kidnaps an elf. A big fight begins.

I think … sounds interesting/boring/funny.

I like /don't like stories about …

Mini Project Authors and books

3 **Either**
Check the Internet or your library for facts about a writer for young people.

Anne Fine
Anne Fine was born in England. One day she could not go to the library because there was a snowstorm. So she started to write novels …

Or
Write a short summary of a book that you have read and enjoyed.

A book that I really enjoyed was 'A Hat full of Sky' by Terry Pratchett. It's about a girl called Tiffany Aching who wants to be a witch …

CLIL

Aurora Borealis - the Northern Lights

KEY WORDS

cosmic weather	North / South Pole	moon	oxygen
high temperature	solar / lunar eclipse	phenomenon	nitrogen
particles	lightning	electric fields	oval-shaped
magnetic field	meteor	gas	

1 Read the texts.

The photos on this page show a 'natural laser show', the Northern Lights. You can see this light show in many different countries in the world, for example, Norway, Finland, Iceland, Canada and Alaska. The Northern Lights are clearest during winter nights. During these nights, the sky often turns red, green, blue or violet. Although we cannot always see them, the auroras are always there. They cover the North and South Pole and are oval-shaped.

The Finnish name for the Northern lights is 'revontulet', which means 'fox fires'. The name comes from an old story. It says that the arctic fox throws up snow with its big bushy tail. The snow goes high up into the sky and starts a fire, the 'fox fire'.

Some Inuit, the native people of Alaska, were very scared of the Northern Lights. They thought they were very dangerous, especially for children. They told their children not to go outside when they were in the sky. They thought the Northern Lights would kill the children!

2a **Read the text.**

What causes the different colours?

Auroras are always two colours: blue and red or green and red. The colours of the aurora depend on different gases in the atmosphere. Nitrogen causes the red and blue lights and oxygen the red and green lights. There is more nitrogen gas in the atmosphere nearer the earth's surface. That is why the sky sometimes looks very red, almost like it's on fire.

2b **Look at the pictures of the Northern Lights on page 154. Decide if the main gas is nitrogen or oxygen.**

Mini Project

3 **Complete the explanations of four other phenomena by using one of the words below to fill the gap.**

rainbow	sun	lightning	moon

1 When there is a solar eclipse, the .... goes in front of the sun.

2 When there is a lunar eclipse, the earth is between the moon and the sun. The earth's shadow falls on the .... so we cannot see it.

3 A .... happens when it is raining and the light of the sun shines on the raindrops.

4 .... happens when ice crystals and water drops in the air bump together to cause electricity.

4 **Choose one of the phenomena in 3. In small groups, draw a diagram to show how the phenomenon works. Use the Internet or a library to help you.**

WORDLIST

U6/10 = Unit 6 Exercise 10; E1 = Story of the Stones Episode 1; NYC2 = Kids in NYC2;
G = Grammar; F = Fido; MORE 1 = Wörter, die schon in MORE 1 vorgekommen sind

A

abracadabra U13/6	[abrəkə dabrə]	Zauberspruch
above MORE 1	[ə'bʌv]	über
accident MORE 1	['æksɪdənt]	Unfall
ache U15/1	[eɪk]	Schmerz(en)
acrobat U11/3	['ækrəbæt]	Akrobat/in
act (it out) U3/4	[ækt]	spielen
action U1/2	['ækʃn]	Handlung; Aktion, Action
activity U7/7	[æk'tɪvəti]	Aktivität
actually U11/2	['æktʃuəli]	eigentlich; tatsächlich
AD (Anno Domini) U7/7	[eɪ'di:]	n. Chr.
address (pl -es) U2/2	[ə'dres]	Adresse, Anschrift
adult MORE 1	['ædʌlt]	Erwachsene/r
adventure MORE 1	[əd'ventʃə]	Abenteuer, Erlebnis
I'm afraid (so)/(not) U14/E6	[aɪm,ə'freɪd]	leider/leider nicht
after all U16/4	[ɑ:ftər'ɔ:l]	schließlich
against U1/9	[ə'gentst]	gegen
age U4/4	[eɪdʒ]	Alter
aged (11) U4/3	[eɪdʒd]	(11) Jahre alt
(two days) ago MORE 1	[ə'gəʊ]	vor (zwei Tagen)
air U1/7	[eə]	Luft
airport U3/1	['eəpɔ:t]	Flughafen
alarm U2/2	[ə'lɑ:m]	Angst; hier: Alarm
alive U4/E2	[ə'laɪv]	lebendig, am Leben
all day U4/2	['ɔ:l deɪ]	den ganzen Tag
all the time U7/3	['ɔ:l ðə 'taɪm]	die ganze Zeit
almost U5/13	['ɔ:lməʊst]	fast, beinahe
along MORE 1	[ə'lɒŋ]	entlang, mit
already U16/6	[ɔ:l'redi]	schon
altar U11/2	['ɔ:ltə]	Altar
aluminium U14/1	[ælə'mɪniəm]	Aluminium
amazing U5/1	[ə'meɪzɪŋ]	erstaunlich
ambulance MORE 1	['æmbjʊləns]	Krankenwagen
an U2/2	[æn]	ein e, r, s
ancient U11/2	['eɪnʃənt]	alt, antik
anecdote U12/12	[ænɪk dəʊt]	Anekdote
ankle U15/2	['æŋkl]	(Fuß)knöchel
another MORE 1	[ə'nʌðə]	noch eine(r, s); ein andere(r, s)
antelope U5/10	['æntɪləʊp]	Antilope
any MORE 1	['eni]	irgendein/e
(not) any longer U14/6	[nɒt'eni lɒŋə]	nicht mehr
(not) any more U7/6	[nɒt'eni 'mɔ:]	nicht mehr
anybody U12/4	['enibɒdi]	jeder; ein jeder
anywhere U20/4	['eniweə]	überall(hin); irgendwo(hin)
apologise, apologize (AE) U19/7	[ə'pɒlədʒaɪz]	sich entschuldigen
appear U18/7	[ə'pɪə]	erscheinen
applause U2/2	[ə'plɔ:z]	Beifall
area U7/3	['eəriə]	Gebiet, Region
argument U20/3	['ɑ:gjʊmənt]	Wortwechsel; Streit
armchair U14/3	['ɑ:mtʃeə]	Sessel, Lehnstuhl
arrest U2/2	[ə'rest]	verhaften
art U1/5	[ɑ:t]	Kunst
article U2/3	['ɑ:tɪkl]	Artikel
as ... as ... MORE 1	[əz əz]	(genau)so ... wie ...
as well U15/1	[əz wel]	auch, ebenfalls
(fall) asleep U18/7	[fɔ:l ə sli:p]	einschlafen
assembly U20/3	[ə'sembli]	Versammlung
assistant U2/1	[ə'sɪstənt]	Assistent/in
(not) at all U6/3	[ət ɔ:l]	gar nicht
Atlantian U5/6	[ət'læntɪən]	Bewohner(in) von Atlantis
attacker U1/9	[ə'tækə]	Angreifer/in
Australia U1/7	[ɒ streɪliə]	Australien
aunt U12/1	['ɑ:nt]	Tante
aunty (informal) MORE 1	['ɑ:nti]	Tantchen
average U19/8	['ævərɪdʒ]	durchschnittlich
awesome U16/1	['ɔ:səm]	beeindruckend

B

back U1/12	[bæk]	Rücken
background U2/2	[bækgraʊnd]	Hintergrund
bacon U8/7	['beɪkən]	Speck
bandage U11/10	['bændɪdʒ]	Verband
bank U6/2; U7/E3	[bæŋk]	Bank; Ufer
barefoot U11/3	['beəfʊt]	barfuß
bark U9/5	[bɑ:k]	bellen
base U18/9	[beɪs]	Fuß, Basis
bat U10/NYC2	[bæt]	Schläger
bath U11/2	[bɑ:θ]	Bad
bathing suit U19/7	['beɪðɪŋ su:t]	Badeanzug
bathroom MORE 1	['bɑ:θru:m]	Bad(ezimmer)
battery U6/6	['bætəri]	Batterie
battle U16/4	['bætl]	Kampf, Schlacht
beach MORE 1	[bi:tʃ]	Strand
bean MORE 1	[bi:n]	Bohne
bear MORE 1	[beə]	Bär
beard MORE 1	[bɪəd]	Bart
beat U14/E6	[bi:t]	schlagen
Beat it! MORE 1	['bi:t,ɪt]	Hau ab!
become MORE 1	[bɪ'kʌm]	werden
bedside table U14/3	['bedsaɪd 'teɪbl]	Nachttisch
beer U13/6	[bɪə]	Bier
behave U17/7	[bɪ heɪv]	sich benehmen
behind MORE 1	[bɪ'haɪnd]	hinter
believe MORE 1	[bɪ'li:v]	glauben
bell U20/4	[bel]	Glocke; Klingel
belong U6/3	[bɪ lɒŋ]	gehören

below U19/8	[bɪ'ləʊ]	unten; unterhalb
belt U4/E2	[belt]	Gürtel
beside U6/G	[bɪ'saɪd]	neben
between U3/1	[bɪ'twi:n]	zwischen
bike MORE 1	[baɪk]	Fahrrad
bird U5/6	[bɜ:d]	Vogel
birdman U18/9	['bɜ:dmæn]	Vogelmensch
give birth to U12/3	[gɪv 'bɜ:θ tə]	zur Welt bringen
bite U1/7	[baɪt]	Biss; beißen
bleep U16/4	[bli:p]	piepsen
block U11/6	[blɒk]	Block, Klotz
blonde U6/8	[blɒnd]	blond
blood U2/2	[blʌd]	Blut
blouse MORE 1	[blaʊz]	Bluse
bob U4/1	[bɒb]	auf und ab hüpfen
apple-bobbing U4/1	['æpl ˌbɒbɪŋ]	Apfeltauchen (traditionelles Halloween-Spiel)
body U11/2	['bɒdi]	Körper
bone U4/F	[bəʊn]	Knochen
boot, car boot U13/5	['kɑ: bu:t]	Kofferraum
boot U20/1	[bu:t]	Stiefel
(be) born U11/10	[bɔ:n]	geboren
borrow (from) U12/9	['bɒrəʊ]	ausleihen (von)
boss someone around (informal) U17/7	[bɒs]	jemanden herumkommandieren
both U13/9	[bəʊθ]	beide
bottle U7/7	['bɒtl]	Flasche
bottom U7/2	['bɒtam]	unten
bowl U10/7	[bəʊl]	Schüssel
branch MORE 1	[brɑ:ntʃ]	Zweig; Ast
brand-new MORE 1	[brænd'nju:]	(funkel) nagelneu
Brazil U18/12	[brə'zɪl]	Brasilien
break U1/6	[breɪk]	Pause
break into U2/2	['breɪk ˌɪntə]	einbrechen in
bridge MORE 1	[brɪdʒ]	Brücke
bright U1/9	[braɪt]	hell, leuchtend
Britain U13/2	['brɪtən]	Großbritannien
British U18/10	['brɪtɪʃ]	britische (r, s)
broom U9/5	[bru:m]	Besen
brush U17/1	[brʌʃ]	(ab)bürsten
buffalo (pl buffaloes) MORE 1	['bʌfələʊ, bʌfələʊz]	Büffel
build U7/3	[bɪld]	bauen
building MORE 1	[bɪldɪŋ]	Gebäude, Bau
bumblebee bat U5/9	['bʌmblbi: bæt]	Hummelfledermaus
bump into ... MORE 1	[bʌmp ˌ'ɪntə]	mit ... zusammenstoßen
bungalow U14/1	['bʌŋgələʊ]	Bungalow
busy MORE 1	['bɪzi]	beschäftigt
button U9/12	['bʌtn]	Knopf
buy MORE 1	[baɪ]	kaufen
buzzer MORE 1	['bʌzə]	Summer, Buzzer
by MORE 1	[baɪ]	bei, mit
by the way U10/NYC2	[baɪ ðə weɪ]	übrigens
bye MORE 1	[baɪ]	tschüss

C

cabbage U10/1	['kæbɪdʒ]	Kohl, Kraut
cache U7/7	[kæʃ]	Versteck
cafeteria MORE 1	[kæfə'tɪəriə]	Cafeteria
cage MORE 1	[keɪdʒ]	Käfig
California U14/1	[kælɪ'fɔrnjə]	Kalifornien
calm down U9/E4	[kɑ:m 'daʊn]	sich beruhigen
camera U9/2	['kæmərə]	Kamera, Fotoapparat
camp U7/3	[kæmp]	Zeltlager
canary U11/10	[kə'neəri]	Kanarienvogel
cancer U15/9	['kænsə]	Krebs (Krankheit)
candle U4/3	['kændl]	Kerze
canoe U7/10	['kənu:]	Kanu, Paddelboot
canoeing U7/3	[kə'nu:ɪŋ]	Paddeln, Kanufahren
car park U3/1	['kɑ: pɑ:k]	Parkplatz
caravan U14/1	['kærəvæn]	Wohnwagen(anhänger)
carbon U18/9	['kɑ:bən]	Kohlenstoff-
care about ... U12/8	['keərˌə'baʊt]	sich aus ... etw. machen
care for U17/9	['keə fə]	sich kümmern um
careful MORE 1	['keəfl]	vorsichtig
carpet U14/3	['kɑ:pɪt]	Teppich
carry U5/9	['kæri]	tragen; hier: übertragen
carry home MORE 1	['kærɪˌ'həʊm]	nach Hause tragen
case MORE 1	[keɪs]	Fall; Hülle
cathedral U11/2	[kə'θi:drəl]	Kathedrale, Dom
cattle U11/3	['kætl]	Vieh
cave U16/2	[keɪv]	Höhle
cell phone U20/NYC4	[sel fəʊn]	Handy
centre U11/12	['sentə]	Zentrum, Mitte
certainly MORE 1	['sɜ:tnli]	sicher(lich); bestimmt
chain U13/1	[tʃeɪn]	Kette
challenge U18/9	['tʃælɪndʒ]	Herausforderung
change MORE 1	[tʃeɪndʒ]	(sich) (ver)ändern
character U2/2	['kærɪktə]	Charakter; hier: Person
chase MORE 1	[tʃeɪs]	verfolgen, jagen
chat U12/9	[tʃæt]	plaudern, chatten; Unterhaltung, Plauderei, Chat
check out U16/4	[tʃek aʊt]	überprüfen
cheek U11/10	[tʃi:k]	Wange, Backe
Cheer up! MORE 1	[tʃɪər 'ʌp]	Lass den Kopf nicht hängen!, Kopf hoch!
cheesecake U10/1	['tʃi:zkeɪk]	Käsekuchen
cheetah U5/9	['tʃi:tə]	Gepard
chef U10/7	[ʃef]	Koch/Köchin
chemist's U6/2	['kemɪst]	Apotheke, Drogerie
chess U20/3	[tʃes]	Schach(spiel)
child, children MORE 1	[tʃaɪld, 'tʃɪldrən]	Kind, Kinder
chimpanzee U5/6	[tʃɪmpæn'zi:]	Schimpanse
choose U11/9	[tʃu:z]	auswählen
chop U10/7	[tʃɒp]	Kotelett
church U6/2	[tʃɜ:tʃ]	Kirche

cigar U13/6	[sɪ'gɑ:]	Zigarre
classmate U6/6	['klɑ:smeɪt]	Klassenkamerad/in, Mitschüler/in
clean U2/2	[kli:n]	sauber; sauber machen, reinigen, putzen
cleaning lady U3/3	['kli:nɪŋ 'leɪdi]	Putzfrau
clear up U19/3	[klɪər 'ʌp]	(auf)klären; hier: sich aufhellen
click U6/6	[klɪk]	Klick
climb MORE 1	[klaɪm]	(hinauf)steigen; klettern
clothes (no pl) MORE 1	['kləʊðz]	Kleider, Kleidung
cloud U19/1	[klaʊd]	Wolke
clue MORE 1	[klu:]	Hinweis, Anhaltspunkt; Tipp
coast U18/9	[kəʊst]	Küste
coat U3/1	[kəʊt]	Mantel
coffee U3/1	['kɒfi]	Kaffee
coin U7/7	[kɔɪn]	Münze, Geldstück
collect MORE 1	[kə'lekt]	sammeln
come true MORE 1	[kʌm 'tru:]	wahr werden
come up to MORE 1	[kʌm 'ʌp tə]	hinkommen auf
comfortable U9/12	['kʌmftəbl]	bequem
command MORE 1	[kə'mɑ:nd]	Befehl
compare U6/9	[kəm'peər]	vergleichen
competition U18/5	[kɒmpə'tɪʃn]	Wettbewerb
complete U3/1	[kəm'pli:t]	vollständig; vervollständigen
complicated U20/3	['kɒmplɪkeɪtɪd]	kompliziert; schwierig
compliment U10/F	['kɒmplɪmənt]	Kompliment
concentrate MORE 1	['kɒnsntreɪt]	(sich) konzentrieren
connect U14/1	[kə'nekt]	anschließen; verbinden
continue U19/1	[kən'tɪnju:]	andauern; weitergehen
control U16/2	[kən'trəʊl]	Kontrolle
conversation U14/7	[kɒnvə'seɪʃn]	Gespräch, Unterhaltung
convert U19/8	[kənvɜ:t]	umwandeln
cook MORE 1	[kʊk]	Koch/Köchin; kochen
cooker U13/5	['kʊkə]	Herd
coordinate U7/7	[kəʊ'ɔ:dɪnət]	Koordinate
corridor U11/14	['kɒrɪdɔ:]	Flur, Gang, Korridor
costume U4/8	['kɒstju:m]	Tracht; Kostüm
could U7/7	[kʊd]	könnte(n)
count MORE 1	[kaʊnt]	zählen
count up MORE 1	[kaʊnt 'ʌp]	hochzählen, zusammenzählen
main course U10/7	['meɪn kɔ:s]	Hauptgericht, Hauptgang
cousin U12/1	['kʌzn]	Cousin/e
cover U1/12	['kʌvə]	bedecken
crash U8/9	[kræʃ]	zu Bruch fahren
create U17/9	[kri'eɪt]	erschaffen, kreieren
creature U16/6	['kri:tʃə]	Kreatur, Lebewesen
cross U6/1; U11/2	[krɒs]	durchqueren, überqueren; Kreuz
cruelty U17/9	['kru:əlti]	Grausamkeit
cry U7/E3	[kraɪ]	Schrei; weinen; schreien
cup U3/1	[kʌp]	Tasse
cup-holder U3/1	['kʌp 'həʊldə]	Becherhalter (z.B. im Auto)
cupboard U14/3	['kʌbəd]	Schrank
curse U11/1	[kɜ:s]	Fluch
curtain U14/3	['kɜ:tən]	Vorhang
cut MORE 1	[kʌt]	schneiden
cycle U18/1	['saɪkl]	Rad fahren

D

damn (informal) U12/12	[dæm]	verdammt
dancer U11/3	['dɑ:nsə]	Tänzer/in
danger U4/E2	['deindʒə]	Gefahr
dangerous U1/9	['deɪndʒərəs]	gefährlich
dare MORE 1	[deə]	herausfordern; sich trauen
dark MORE 1	[dɑ:k]	Dunkelheit; dunkel
daughter MORE 1	['dɔ:tə]	Tochter
dead U14/E6	[ded]	tot
deckchair U13/5	['dektʃeə]	Liegestuhl
deep U5/G	[di:p]	tief
definitely U18/6	['defənətli]	eindeutig, definitiv; auf jeden Fall
degree (°) U19/3	[dɪ'gri:]	Grad (°)
delete U12/9	[dɪ'li:t]	streichen, löschen
delta U11/2	['deltə]	Delta, Flussmündung
demon U4/E2	['di:mən]	Dämon
depend U5/NYC1	[dɪpend]	abhängen von
desert U5/9	['dezət]	Wüste
design and technology U1/5	[dɪ'zaɪn ənd tek'nɒlədʒi]	Design und technisches Zeichnen
desk MORE 1	[desk]	Schreibtisch
dessert U10/2	[dɪ'zɜ:t]	Nachtisch, Dessert
destroy U12/E5	[dɪ'strɔɪ]	zerstören
diamond U20/1	['daɪəmənd]	Diamant
diary U20/3	[daɪəri]	Tagebuch
dictionary U14/7	['dɪkʃənəri]	Wörterbuch
die U5/9	[daɪ]	sterben
different MORE 1	['dɪfrənt]	anders, andere (r, s); verschieden
difficult MORE 1	['dɪfɪklt]	schwierig, schwer
dig MORE 1	[dɪg]	graben
dinner lady MORE 1	['dɪnə 'leɪdi]	Serviererin am Schulbuffet
directions U6/10	[dɪrekʃəns]	Anweisungen
dirty U2/2	['dɜ:ti]	dreckig, schmutzig
disappear U4/6	[dɪsə'pɪə]	verschwinden
disappointed U15/1	[dɪsə'pɔɪntɪd]	enttäuscht
discover U11/10	[dɪ'skʌvə]	herausfinden, entdecken
the dishes (pl) U12/8	[ðə 'dɪʃɪz]	das Geschirr

doctor U2/2	['dɒktə]	Arzt/Ärztin
document U11/3	['dɒkjʊmənt]	Dokument
dolphin U5/10	['dɒlfɪn]	Delphin
done MORE 1	[dʌn]	fertig
doom U16/2	[du:m]	Verhängnis
doorbell U13/6	['dɔ:bel]	Türklingel
double MORE 1	['dʌbl]	doppelt, Doppel-
down MORE 1	[daʊn]	hinunter, hinab
dragon MORE 1	['drægən]	Drache
draw U19/4	['drɔ:]	malen; zeichnen
drawer MORE 1	['drɔ:ə]	Schublade
drawing U9/8	[drɔ:ɪŋ]	Zeichnung
dream U2/1	[dri:m]	Traum; träumen
dress MORE 1	[dres]	Kleid
drive U3/1; U4/4; U8/9	[draɪv]	Laufwerk; Einfahrt; Fahrt
driving test U8/9	[draɪvɪŋ test]	Fahrprüfung
drop U15/5L	[drɒp]	fallen lassen
drummer MORE 1	['drʌmə]	Trommler/in, Schlagzeuger/in
drums MORE 1	[drʌmz]	Schlagzeug
dry U17/1; U19/8	[draɪ]	trocknen; trocken
dustbin U9/5	['dʌstbɪn]	Mülleimer

E

each other U14/4	[i:tʃ ʌðər]	einander, gegenseitig
eagle MORE 1	['i:gl]	Adler
early MORE 1	['ɜ:li]	früh
earth U4/E2	[ɜ:θ]	Erde
east U5/9	[i:st]	östlich, Ost-; Osten
education U18/10	[edjʊ'keɪʃn]	(Aus)bildung
Egypt MORE 1	['i:dʒɪpt]	Ägypten
Egyptian U11/2	[ɪ'dʒɪpʃən]	Ägypter/in; ägyptisch
eldest U12/4	['eldəst]	älteste(r, s)
electricity U14/1	[ɪlek'trɪsəti]	Elektrizität, Strom
something else U7/7	[sʌmθɪŋ'els]	noch etwas
emergency MORE 1	[ɪ'mɜ:dʒənsi]	Notfall, Notdienst
emperor, empress U11/2	['empərə, 'emprəs]	Kaiser, Kaiserin
empty MORE 1	['empti]	leer
ending U11/15	['endɪŋ]	Ende, Schluss
endless U16/4	['endləs]	endlos
English channel U18/9	['ɪŋglɪʃ 'tʃænəl]	Ärmelkanal
Englishman (pl -men) U11/8	['ɪŋglɪʃmən, ɪŋglɪʃmən]	Engländer
enjoy MORE 1	[ɪndʒɔɪ]	genießen
enough MORE 1	[ɪ'nʌf]	genügend, ausreichend, genug
escape U9/E4	[ɪ'skeɪp]	(ent)fliehen; entkommen
especially U7/7	[ɪ'speʃli]	besonders
etc. (et cetera) U20/3	[et 'setərə]	usw., etc.
even U11/3	['i:vən]	sogar
even U12/3	['i:vən]	nicht mal
even U19/8	['i:vən]	noch
ever U18/5	['evə]	je
every MORE 1	['evri]	jede(r, s)
everybody MORE 1	['evribɒdi]	jede(r); alle
everyone U1/7	['evriwʌn]	jede(r); alle
everything MORE 1	['evriθɪŋ]	alles
everywhere U1/1	['evriweə]	überall
exactly U7/7	[ɪg'zæktli]	genau
for example U7/7	[fər ɪg'zɑ:mpl]	zum Beispiel
excited MORE 1	[ɪk'saɪtɪd]	aufgeregt
exciting MORE 1	[ɪk'saɪtɪŋ]	aufregend; spannend
exotic U5/6	[ɪg'zɒtɪk]	exotisch; fremdländisch
experiment U2/2	[ɪk'sperɪmənt]	Experiment, Versuch
explain U3/5	[ɪk'spleɪn]	erklären
explode U9/3	[ɪks'pləʊd]	explodieren
expression U7/E3	[ɪkspreʃən]	Ausdruck
extra U3/4	['ekstrə]	mehr; besonders; Extra
extreme U18/9	[ɪk'stri:m]	extrem

F

face MORE 1	[feɪs]	sich zuwenden, ins Auge sehen
fact U2/2	[fækt]	Tatsache, Fakt; Wirklichkeit
(it isn't) fair U10/NYC2	[ɪt izənt feə]	Es ist nicht fair.
fall over U11/14	[fɔ:l 'əʊvə]	hinfallen; umfallen
famous MORE 1	['feɪməs]	berühmt
fancy dress U8/13	['fænsi 'dres]	Verkleidung, Kostüm
farewell U14/E6	[feə'wel]	Abschied
farmer U11/3	['fɑ:mə]	Bauer/Bäuerin, Farmer/in
fat U11/3; U17/7	[fæt]	Fett; fett
fault U12/E5	[fɔ:lt]	Schuld
favour, favor (AE) U5/NYC1	[feɪvə]	Gefallen
favourite MORE 1	['feɪvərət]	Lieblings-
fearless U18/9	['fɪələs]	furchtlos
feather U13/5	['feðə]	Feder
feed MORE 1	[fi:d]	zu essen geben, füttern
fence U13/5	[fens]	Zaun
few U10/NYC2	[fju:]	ein paar; einige
field U7/1	[fi:ld]	Feld
fight U16/6	[faɪt]	kämpfen
file U12/9	[faɪl]	(Akten)hefter, Ordner
fill U13/6	[fɪl]	füllen
fill in U10/12	[fɪl ɪn]	eintragen
final U15/12	['faɪnəl]	Finale
finally MORE 1	['faɪn(ə)li]	schließlich; endlich
find out U7/7	[faɪnd 'aʊt]	herausfinden
fingerprint U2/2	['fɪŋgəprɪnt]	Fingerabdruck
finish U13/9	['fɪnɪʃ]	beenden; vervollständigen
fire brigade U3/F	['faɪə brɪ'geɪd]	Feuerwehr
fire chief U3/1	['faɪə tʃi:f]	Brandmeister
firefighter U3/F	['faɪəfaɪtə]	Feuerwehrmann/ Feuerwehrfrau
fireman (pl firemen) U3/5	['faɪəmən, faɪəmən]	Feuerwehrmann/ Feuerwehrfrau

fishing rod MORE 1	[fɪʃɪŋ rɒd]	Angelrute
flash U16/4	[flæʃ]	blitzen
flee U1/1	[fli:]	flüchten
flight U3/1	[flaɪt]	Fliegen; Flug
float U13/1	[fləʊt]	schwimmen, oben bleiben
floor U2/1; U14/1	[flɔ:]	Boden; Stockwerk
flower U6/8	['flaʊə]	Blume
fog U19/2	[fɒg]	Nebel
follow MORE 1	['fɒləʊ]	folgen
be fond (of) MORE 1	[fɒnd]	(etw.) gerne mögen
fool U1/1	[fu:l]	Narr
footprint U2/2	['fʊtprɪnt]	Fußabdruck
for sure U12/E5	[fə 'ʃɔ:]	bestimmt, ganz(informal) sicher
forbid U16/4	[fə'bɪd]	verbieten
force U16/6	[fɔ:s]	Gewalt
forecast U19/3	[fɔ:ka:st]	Vorhersage
forest U6/1	['fɒrɪst]	Wald
forgetful U12/12	[fə'getfəl]	vergesslich
fork U10/5	[fɔ:k]	Gabel
formula U19/1	['fɔ:mjələ]	Formel
free MORE 1	[fri:]	befreien; frei, kostenlos
free fall U18/9	[fri: 'fɔ:l]	freier Fall
freedom MORE 1	['fri:dəm]	Freiheit, Unabhängigkeit
freeze MORE 1	[fri:z]	gefrieren; einfrieren
fridge MORE 1	[frɪdʒ]	Kühlschrank
friendly U5/6	['frendli]	freundlich
front U3/1	[frʌnt]	Vorderseite
in front (of) U16/4	[ɪn 'frʌnt]	vor
front door MORE 1	[frʌnt 'dɔ:]	Vordertür; Haustür
funny U3/7	[fʌni]	lustig, komisch
furious U1/12	['fjʊəriəs]	wütend
future U16/2	['fju:tʃə]	zukünftig

G

gamemaster U16/2	['geɪmma:stə]	Spielleiter
gaming cards U5/6	[geɪmɪŋ ka:ds]	Spielkarten
garage U13/6	['gæra:ʒ]	Garage
gas U9/E4	[gæs]	Gas
gate U4/4	[geɪt]	Tor
generally U19/8	['dʒenərəli]	im Allgemeinen
genius U12/12	['dʒi:niəs]	Genie
gentleman (pl gentlemen) U2/2	['dʒentlmən, 'dʒentlmən]	Gentleman; Herr
geo-caching U7/7	[dʒi:əʊkæʃɪŋ]	Geo-caching, GPS-Schnitzeljagd
geography U1/5	['dʒɒgrəfi]	Erdkunde, Geografie
get MORE 1	[get]	erhalten, bekommen; holen
(I don't) get (it) U20/NYC4	[aɪ dəʊnt get ɪt]	Verstehe ich nicht.
get in touch U2/E1	[get ɪn tʌtʃ]	sich kontaktieren, sich in Verbindung setzen
get lost U18/5	[get 'lɒst]	sich verirren; sich verlaufen haben
get married U12/3	[get 'mærɪd]	heiraten
get out (of) MORE 1	[get 'aʊt əv]	hinauskommen/ herauskommen (aus)
get stuck U20/1	[get 'stʌk]	festsitzen
get together U12/13	[get təgeðə]	zusammenkommen
get up MORE 1	[get 'ʌp]	aufstehen
Get well soon! U15/12	['get wel 'su:n]	Gute Besserung!
ghost U4/1	[gəʊst]	Geist
giraffe U5/10	[dʒə'ra:f]	Giraffe
girlfriend U2/2	['gɜ:lfrend]	Freundin
give up U14/E6	[gɪv ʌp]	aufgeben
glad U13/6	[glæd]	froh
go for a walk U17/8	[gəʊ fɔ:r ə wɔ:k]	spazieren gehen
go off U2/2	[gəʊ 'ɒf]	losgehen, weggehen; abgehen; ausgehen
go on MORE 1	[gəʊ 'ɒn]	weitergehen; weitermachen
go red U20/3	[gəʊ 'red]	rot werden
go to sleep MORE 1	[gəʊ tə 'sli:p]	einschlafen
goal U15/G	[gəʊl]	Tor
goalie (informal) U18/8	['gəʊli]	Tormann, Torfrau
goat U11/3	[gəʊt]	Ziege
god U11/8	[gɒd]	Gott
golf U1/9	[gɒlf]	Golf
good-looking U13/8	[gʊd 'lʊkɪŋ]	gutaussehend
goose (pl geese) U11/2	[gu:s, gi:s]	Gans
Got you! U20/NYC4	[gɒt jʊ]	Hab' dich!
gram U5/9	[græm]	Gramm
grandchild (pl -children) U12/3	['græntʃaɪld, 'græntʃɪldrən]	Enkelkind
granddad PC 11-15	[grændæd]	Großvater
grandparents (pl) U12/7	[grænpeərənts]	Großeltern
grape U10/1	[greɪp]	Traube
graphics (no pl) U16/1	['græfɪks]	Grafik
great-grandchild (pl -children) U12/3	[greɪt'græntʃaɪld, greɪt'græntʃɪldrən]	Urenkelkind
grilled U15/NYC3	[grɪld]	gegrillt
ground MORE 1	[graʊnd]	(Erd)boden, Erde
group U11/12	[gru:p]	Gruppe
grow U5/13	[grəʊ]	wachsen; hier: werden
grow up U16/4	[grəʊ ʌp]	aufwachsen
guard U2/2; U11/8	[ga:d]	Wache; Wach(t) posten; bewachen
guess MORE 1	[ges]	(er)raten
guest MORE 1	[gest]	Gast
guide U7/3	[gaɪd]	(Reise)führer, Reiseleiter
gun U2/5	[gʌn]	Schusswaffe
guy MORE 1	[gaɪ]	Kerl, Typ
guys (informal) MORE 1	[gaɪz]	Leute
gymnastics (pl) U1/2	[dʒɪm'næstɪks]	Turnen

H

hairy U5/4	['heəri]	haarig, stark behaart
Halloween U4/1	[hæləʊi:n]	Halloween
ham U10/4	[hæm]	Schinken
handful U7/7	['hændfʊl]	eine Hand voll
hang on U5/NYC1	[hæŋ 'ɒn]	durchhalten; hier: warten
happen U2/2	[hæpən]	geschehen
hard U18/9	[hɑ:d]	hart
hard hat U7/3	['hɑ:d hæt]	Schutzhelm
harmless U16/2	['hɑ:mləs]	harmlos
haunted U4/1	['hɔ:ntɪd]	Spuk-
Have fun! U15/NYC3	[hæv fʌn]	Viel Spaß!
hay MORE 1	[heɪ]	Heu
headache U15/1	['hedeɪk]	Kopfschmerzen
headmaster U20/3	[hed'mɑ:stə]	Schulleiter, Rektor
healthy U17/9	['helθi]	gesund
hear MORE 1	[hɪə]	hören
heat U14/1	[hi:t]	Wärme; Hitze
heaven MORE 1	['hevn]	Himmel
heavy U5/1	['hevi]	schwer
height U18/9	[haɪt]	Höhe
helmet U16/2	['helmɪt]	Helm
Here we go! MORE 1	[hɪə wi: 'gəʊ]	Jetzt geht"s los!
Here you are. MORE 1	[hɪə ju: 'ɑ:]	Hier, bitte!, Bitte schön!
hers U14/7	[hɜ:z]	ihre(r, s)
hieroglyphics U11/1	[haɪrə'glɪfɪks]	Hieroglyphen
high U5/13	[haɪ]	hoch
hill U17/7	[hɪl]	Hügel; Anhöhe
hire MORE 1	['haɪə]	mieten, ausleihen
history U1/5	['hɪstəri]	Geschichte
hold MORE 1	[həʊld]	(fest)halten
hold up MORE 1	[həʊld 'ʌp]	nach oben halten
holder U3/1	['həʊldə]	Halter
hole MORE 1	[həʊl]	Loch
hook MORE 1	[hʊk]	Haken
hop U2/2	[hɒp]	hüpfen
hopefully U12/E5	['həʊpfəli]	hoffnungsvoll; hoffentlich
horn U11/3	[hɔ:n]	Horn
horse MORE 1	[hɔ:s]	Pferd
how to U13/2	['haʊ tə]	wie man
hug U1/12	[hʌg]	umarmen
huge U9/3	[hju:dʒ]	riesig, riesengroß
human U11/2	['hju:mən]	Mensch; menschlich
hunt U1/9	[hʌnt]	jagen; jagd
hurray U13/2	[hʊ'reɪ]	hurra
hurricane U18/10	['hʌrɪkən]	Orkan; Hurrikan
hurt MORE 1	[hɜ:t]	wehtun, schmerzen;
husband MORE 1	['hʌzbənd]	Ehemann
hut MORE 1	[hʌt]	Hütte
hypnotise U2/1	['hɪpnətaɪz]	hypnotisieren
hypnotist U2/1	['hɪpnətɪst]	Hypnotiseur, Hypnotisiererin

I

ice U18/1	[aɪs]	Eis
ice skating U18/1	['aɪsskeɪtɪŋ]	Schlittschuh laufen
I'd like U10/5	[aɪd laɪk]	ich möchte
if U20/4	[ɪf]	wenn
ill MORE 1	[ɪl]	krank
illness U15/9	['ɪlnəs]	Krankheit
imagine U7/11	[ɪ'mædʒɪn]	sich vorstellen
important U11/2	[ɪm'pɔ:tənt]	wichtig
in fact U19/8	[ɪn 'fækt]	genau genommen
inch (pl inches) U19/8	[ɪntʃ, 'ɪntʃɪz]	Zoll (2,54 cm)
incorrect U5/2	[ɪnkərekt]	nicht richtig, falsch
indeed U9/E4	[ɪn'di:d]	in der Tat, wirklich
India U12/7	['ɪndiə]	Indien
Indian U15/9	['ɪndiən]	Indianer/in; indianisch
Indonesia U1/9	['ɪndə'ni:ʒa]	Indonesien
information technology (IT) U1/5	[ɪnfə'meɪʃn tek'nɒlədʒi]	Informatik
ink U1/12	[ɪŋk]	Tinte
instruction U13/F	[ɪn'strʌkʃn]	Anweisung, Instruktion
intelligent U5/12	[ɪn'telɪdʒənt]	intelligent
intention U8/1	[ɪn'tenʃən]	Vorhaben, Absicht
interested (in) U11/10	['ɪntrəstɪd]	interessiert (an)
interesting U3/7	['ɪntrəstɪŋ]	interessant
into MORE 1	['ɪntʊ]	in
invent U11/2	[ɪn'vent]	erfinden
invention U11/2	[ɪn'ventʃən]	Erfindung
invite MORE 1	[ɪn'vaɪt]	einladen

J

jam U11/9	[dʒæm]	Marmelade
Japan U1/7	[dʒə'pæn]	Japan
jewel U2/2	['dʒu:əl]	Juwel
jewellery U1/2	['dʒu:əlri]	Schmuck
join (in) MORE 1	['dʒɔɪn]	teilnehmen (an), mitmachen (bei)
joke U7/7	[dʒəʊk]	Witz
journey U9/3	['dʒɜ:ni]	Reise
juggle MORE 1	[dʒʌgl]	jonglieren
juggler U11/3	['dʒʌglə]	Jongleur/in
jungle U16/1	['dʒʌŋgl]	Dschungel
junior U18/6	['dʒu:niə]	Junior; Junioren-, Jugend-
junk food MORE 1	['dʒʌŋk fu:d]	Schnellgerichte; ungesundes Essen
Just kidding! MORE 1	[dʒʌst 'kɪdɪŋ]	War nur ein Scherz.

K

karate U20/3	[kə'rɑ:ti]	Karate
(be) keen on U4/11	[ki:n]	sich begeistern für
kick U4/11; U18/8	[kɪk]	Tritt, Stoß; treten, kicken
kilogram U11/6	['kɪləgræm]	Kilogramm
what kind (of) MORE 1	[wɒt 'kaɪnd]	was für
kiss U2/2	[kɪs]	küssen
kitchen MORE 1	['kɪtʃən]	Küche
kite U11/2	[kaɪt]	Kite-Drache
knife (pl knives) U10/5	[naɪf, naɪvz]	Messer
knight U4/E2	[naɪt]	Ritter
knock MORE 1	[nɒk]	Klopfen; klopfen
know MORE 1	[nəʊ]	wissen; kennen

L

lake U7/1	[leɪk]	See
lamb U10/1	[læm]	Lamm
lamp U6/G	[læmp]	Lampe
lamp post U6/F	['læmp pəʊst]	Laternenmast
land U5/9; U9/5	[lænd]	Land; landen
language MORE 1	['læŋgwɪdʒ]	Sprache
large U6/3	[lɑ:dʒ]	groß
late MORE 1	[leɪt]	(zu) spät
later MORE 1	['leɪtə]	später
laugh MORE 1	[lɑ:f]	lachen
laughter MORE 1	['lɑ:ftə]	Gelächter
lazy MORE 1	['leɪzi]	faul; träge
leaf (pl leaves) U11/3	[li:f, li:vz]	Blatt
league U16/1	[li:g]	Liga
at least U1/F	[ət 'li:st]	mindestens, wenigstens
(at) least U12/E5	[li:st]	am wenigsten
leather U11/3	['leðə]	Leder
leave MORE 1	[li:v]	verlassen, weggehen
left-hand U7/2	['lefthænd]	linke(r, s)
lemon U10/9	['lemən]	Zitrone
less (than) U15/9	[les]	weniger (als)
let go MORE 1	[let 'gəʊ]	loslassen
Let's see. U15/NYC3	[lets si:]	Schauen wir mal.
library MORE 1	['laɪbrəri]	Bibliothek, Bücherei
lie MORE 1	[laɪ]	liegen; sich legen
life (pl lives) MORE 1	[laɪf, laɪvz]	Leben
life jacket U7/3	['laɪf dʒækɪt]	Schwimmweste
lifetime U12/3	['laɪftaɪm]	Lebenszeit
lift (up) MORE 1	[lɪft]	(hoch)heben
light U11/3; U11/14	[laɪt]	leicht; Licht
list U7/7	[lɪst]	Liste
litter (no pl) U17/1	['lɪtə]	Müll, Abfall
litter tray U17/1	['lɪtə treɪ]	Katzenklo
a little MORE 1	[ə 'lɪtl]	ein bisschen
(door) lock U4/4	['dɔ: lɒk]	(Tür)schloss
lock U13/2	[lɒk]	abschließen
log in U16/2	[lɒg 'ɪn]	sich einloggen
look U11/3	[lʊk]	Blick, Aussehen
look after MORE 1	[lʊk 'ɑ:ftə]	sich kümmern um
look at MORE 1	['lʊk ət]	betrachten, sehen
look for MORE 1	['lʊk fə]	suchen nach
lose U15/G	[lu:z]	verlieren
be lost U4/2	[bi 'lɒst]	sich verirrt haben
a lot (of) MORE 1	[ə 'lɒt (əv)]	viel(e)
lots of MORE 1	['lɒts,əv]	viel, jede Menge
low U6/6	[ləʊ]	niedrig, schwach
be lucky MORE 1	[bi: 'lʌki]	Glück haben
lucky MORE 1	['lʌki]	glücklich

M

mad MORE 1	[mæd]	wahnsinnig; böse
madam U6/4	['mædəm]	gnädige Frau (Anrede)
made of U11/3	[meɪd əv]	aus… gemacht
magic U13/6	['mædʒɪk]	Magie, Zauber
maid MORE 1	[meɪd]	Dienstmädchen
main U6/6	[meɪn]	Haupt-
make fun of ... MORE 1	[meɪk 'fʌn əv]	sich über ... lustig machen
make sure U19/4	[meɪk 'ʃɔ:]	sich versichern, darauf achten
make up U5/16	[meɪk ʌp]	erfinden
make way U3/F	[meɪk 'weɪ]	Platz machen
(shopping) mall U20/4	[mɔ:l]	(große) Einkaufspassage
mammal U5/9	['mæml]	Säugetier
man (pl men) MORE 1	[mæn, men]	Mann
many MORE 1	['meni]	viele
map U6/4	[mæp]	(Land)karte
market U20/NYC4	[mɑ:kɪt]	Markt
married U12/7	['mærɪd]	verheiratet
mask U4/3	[mɑ:sk]	Maske
match U2/E1	[mætʃ]	zuordnen
mathematician U12/12	['mæθəmə'tɪʃn]	Mathematiker/in
It doesn't matter. MORE 1	[ɪt dʌznt 'mætə]	Das ist nicht wichtig.
maximum U19/4	[mæksɪməm]	Maximum
maybe MORE 1	['meɪbi]	vielleicht
mean U4/4	[mi:n]	gemein
mean MORE 1	[mi:n]	bedeuten; meinen
meat U5/14	[mi:t]	Fleisch
medal U2/1	['medl]	Medaille
medicine (no pl) U1/9	[medsn]	Medizin, Medikament(e)
medium U10/5	['mi:diəm]	durchschnittlich, mittel (groß)
meeting U3/1	[mi:tiŋ]	Treffen, Begegnung
melt U11/3	[melt]	schmelzen
memory MORE 1	['mem(ə)ri]	Gedächtnis
menu U10/7	['menju:]	Speisekarte
mess U2/2	[mes]	Unordnung, Durcheinander
messy MORE 1	['mesi]	unordentlich, schlampig
metre U1/1	['mi:tə]	Meter
middle U5/1	['mɪdl]	Mitte
might U8/9	[maɪt]	könnte; vielleicht (tun, sein)
mild U19/8	[maɪld]	sanft; mild
mile U18/10	[maɪl]	Meile
million U11/7	['mɪljən]	Million
mine U14/7	[maɪn]	meine(r, s)
mineral water U10/5	['mɪnərəl 'wɔ:tə]	Mineralwasser
miss U8/9	[mɪs]	vermissen, verpassen
mist U19/3	[mɪst]	Nebel
mobile (phone) U20/NYC4	[məʊbaɪl fəʊn]	Handy
mode U16/6	[məʊd]	Modus
moon U7/1	[mu:n]	Mond
morph MORE 1	[mɔ:f]	morphen, sich verwandeln
mosquito (pl -es or -s) U5/9	[mɒ'ski:təʊ, mɒ'ski:təʊz]	Stechmücke, Moskito
most U7/7	[məʊst]	am meisten; die meisten
most of the time U7/7	['məʊst əv ðə taɪm]	meistens

motor home U14/1	['məʊtə həʊm]	Wohnmobil
motorbike U16/6	['məʊtəbaɪk]	Motorrad
motorway U7/1	['məʊtəweɪ]	Autobahn
mountain U5/6	['maʊntɪn]	Berg
mouse (pl mice) MORE 1	[maʊs, maɪs]	Maus
move U7/5	[mu:v]	(sich) bewegen; umziehen
mummy U11/1	['mʌmi]	Mumie
mushroom U10/4	['mʌʃru:m]	Pilz
musician U11/3	[mju'zɪʃn]	Musiker/in
myself U17/F	[maɪ'self]	mir, mich; hier: selbst

N

nail U13/5	[neɪl]	Nagel
naked U11/3	['neɪkɪd]	nackt, unbekleidet
nasty U13/1	['nɑ:sti]	scheußlich, grässlich, widerlich
national U18/4	['næʃnəl]	national; National-
nearly U16/2	['nɪəli]	fast; beinahe
neck U13/10	[nek]	Hals; Nacken
need U16/4	[ni:d]	brauchen
neighbour MORE 1	['neɪbə]	Nachbar/in
Neither do I. U17/7	['naɪðə dʊ 'aɪ]	Ich auch nicht.
nervous MORE 1	[nɜ:vəs]	nervös
never MORE 1	['nevə]	nie(mals)
news (pl) MORE 1	[nju:z]	Nachrichten
newsagent's MORE 1	['nju:zeɪdʒənts]	Zeitungsgeschäft
newspaper MORE 1	['nju:zpeɪpə]	Zeitung
next door U14/7	[nekst 'dɔ:]	nebenan
nil U18/8	[nɪl]	nichts, null
nineties U13/8	['naɪntiz]	neunziger Jahre
no longer U14/E6	['nəʊ lɒŋə]	nicht mehr
no one U4/2	['nəʊ wʌn]	niemand
nobody MORE 1	['nəʊbədi]	niemand
noise MORE 1	[nɔɪz]	Lärm, Krach; Geräusch
none U14/E6	[nʌn]	keine(r, s)
north U1/7	[nɔ:θ]	nördlich, Nord-; Norden
Northern Ireland U19/4E	['nɔ:ðən 'aɪələnd]	Nordirland
note U7/7	[nəʊt]	Notiz
nothing MORE 1	['nʌθɪŋ]	nichts
notice MORE 1	['nəʊtɪs]	bemerken
nugget MORE 1	['nʌgɪt]	Klumpen

O

object U11/3	['ɒbdʒɪkt]	Objekt, Gegenstand, Sache
ocean U18/10	['əʊʃn]	Meer, Ozean
octopus (pl -es) U1/7	['ɒktəpəs]	Tintenfisch
the odd one out U9/9	[ðɪ 'ɒd wʌn 'aʊt]	das fünfte Rad am Wagen; hier: das Wort, das nicht zu den anderen passt
of course MORE 1	[əv 'kɔ:s]	natürlich
off MORE 1	[ɒf]	aus; weg
office U6/2	['ɒfɪs]	Büro
officer U13/6	['ɒfɪsə]	Offizier/in; Beamtin/Beamter
olive U10/4	['ɒlɪv]	Olive
on his own U1/7	[ɒn hɪs 'əʊn]	allein, auf sich gestellt
on my own U18/8	[ɒn maɪ 'əʊn]	alleine
once MORE 1	[wʌns]	einmal
once upon a time MORE 1	['wʌns əpɒn ə 'taɪm]	es war einmal
one by one U9/3	[wʌn baɪ wʌn]	einer nach dem anderen
onto MORE 1	['ɒntə]	auf
opposite U6/4	['ɒpəzɪt]	gegenüber
order MORE 1; U10/5	['ɔ:də]	bestellen; Reihenfolge
ostrich U5/10	['ɒstrɪtʃ]	(Vogel) Strauß
other U16/2	['ʌðər]	andere, r, s
ours U14/7	['aʊəz]	unsere(r, s)
outdoor U7/1		im Freien
out of MORE 1	['aʊt əv]	aus
outer space U16/4	[aʊtə 'speɪs]	Weltraum, Weltall
outlook U19/3	['aʊtlʊk]	Aussicht
outside MORE 1	[aʊt'saɪd]	außen, außerhalb
over MORE 1	['əʊvə]	über, herüber
owl MORE 1	[aʊl]	Eule
own MORE 1	[əʊn]	eigene(r, s)
owner MORE 1	['əʊnə]	Besitzer/in, Eigentümer/in
ox (pl oxen) U11/3	[ɒks, 'ɒksən]	Ochse
oxygen U15/9	['ɒksɪdʒən]	Sauerstoff

P

pack U19/7	[pæk]	packen
pain U15/1	[peɪn]	Schmerz
paint U3/8	[peɪnt]	malen, streichen
painting U11/3	['peɪntɪŋ]	Bild, Gemälde
pair U12/13	[peər]	Paar
palm (leaves) U11/3	['pɑ:m]	Palmen- (Blätter)
pancake U10/1	['pænkeɪk]	Pfannkuchen
panel U14/1	['pænəl]	Paneel; Blech
papyrus U11/1	[pə'paɪrəs]	Papyrus
parachute U18/9	['pærəʃu:t]	Fallschirm; mit dem Fallschirm abspringen
paragraph U7/10	['pærəgrɑ:f]	Absatz, Abschnitt
Pardon. U8/7	['pɑ:dn]	Entschuldigung!; Wie bitte?
part U9/E4	[pɑ:t]	Teil
partner U6/5	['pɑ:tnə]	Partner/in
pass (a test) U15/G	[pɑ:s]	(eine Prüfung) bestehen
pass through U13/1	[pɑ:s 'θru:]	durchlaufen; hier: durchgehen durch
past U6/1	[pɑ:st]	nach; vorbei an
path U6/1	[pɑ:θ]	Weg, Pfad
pay U11/3	[peɪ]	bezahlen
pea MORE 1	[pi:]	Erbse
peace MORE 1	[pi:s]	Friede
peaceful U17/9	['pi:sfl]	friedlich; friedfertig
peach U10/1	[pi:tʃ]	Pfirsich
peak U19/8	[pi:k]	Gipfel, Bergspitze

pear U10/1	[peə]	Birne
people (pl) MORE 1	['pi:pl]	Leute, Menschen
per cent (%) U11/2	[pə'sent]	Prozent (%)
perfume U11/3	['pɜ:fju:m]	Parfüm
perfumed U11/3	['pɜ:fju:md]	parfümiert
perhaps MORE 1	[pə'hæps]	vielleicht
person U11/5	['pɜ:sn]	Person, Mensch
pharaoh U11/2	['feərəʊ]	Pharaoh
photo U3/1	['fəʊtəʊ]	Foto
photograph U9/2	['fəʊtəgrɑ:f]	Foto(grafie)
physical education (PE) U1/5	['fɪzɪkl, edjʊ'keɪʃn]	Sport(unterricht)
pick up MORE 1	[pɪk 'ʌp]	aufheben, abholen
picnic U7/3	['pɪknɪk]	Picknick
pie U10/1	[paɪ]	Pastete
piece MORE 1	[pi:s]	Stück
pig U5/1	[pɪg]	Schwein
piggy bank MORE 1	['pɪgi bæŋk]	Sparschwein
pill U15/1	[pɪl]	Tablette
pitch (AE) U10/NYC2	[pɪtʃ]	werfen
pity U19/9	['pɪti]	hier: schade, dass
plan U9/4	[plæn]	plane
plan (house) U14/6	[plæn]	Lageplan
plane U1/1	[pleɪn]	Flugzeug
planet U9/3	['plænɪt]	Planet
plant U11/2	[plɑ:nt]	Pflanze
play U2/2	[pleɪ]	Theaterstück; Spiel
play a trick/tricks on somebody U4/3	[pleɪ ə 'trɪk ɒn]	jemanden einen Streich spielen
plum U10/1	[plʌm]	Pflaume
pocket U1/2	['pɒkɪt]	(Hosen-)Tasche
pocket money U1/2	['pɒkɪt 'mʌni]	Taschengeld
point (at) U7/7	[pɔɪnt]	zeigen (auf)
poison U1/9	['pɔɪzn]	Gift
poisonous U1/7	['pɔɪznəs]	giftig
police U2/2	[pə'li:s]	Polizei
pond MORE 1	[pɒnd]	Teich
popular U5/6	['pɒpjʊlə]	beliebt
pork U10/1	[pɔ:k]	Schweinefleisch
portal U16/2	['pɔ:təl]	Portal
Portuguese U12/7	[pɔ:tʃʊ'gi:z]	Portugiese/in; portugiesisch
possible U12/3	['pɒsɪbl]	möglich
post U8/5	[pəʊst]	Post
post office U6/2	['pəʊst ɒfɪs]	Postamt
pot U13/6	[pɒt]	Topf
power U9/E4	['paʊər]	Kraft
powerful U16/2	['paʊəfl]	mächtig
practice MORE 1	[præktɪs]	Übung
practise MORE 1	['præktɪs]	üben; Übung
present MORE 1	['preznt]	Geschenk
president U9/3	['prezɪdənt]	Präsident/in
pretty MORE 1	['prɪti]	hübsch
price MORE 1	[praɪs]	Preis
priest U11/8	[pri:st]	Priester/in
print out U12/9	['prɪnt aʊt]	ausdrucken
prison U13/5	['prɪzn]	Gefängnis
private U12/9	['praɪvət]	privat, Privat-
prize U15/NYC3	[praɪz]	Preis
probably U9/E4	['prɒbəbli]	wahrscheinlich
produce U15/10	[prə'dju:s]	erzeugen
professional U18/6	[prə'feʃnəl]	Fachmann, Fachfrau, Profi; beruflich, Profi-
professor U11/7	[prə'fesə]	Professor/in
profile U18/9	['prəʊfaɪl]	Profil
promise U19/5	['prɒmɪs]	versprechen; Versprechen
pronto U2/2	['prɒntəʊ]	fix
protect U4/E2	[prə'tekt]	schützen
proud MORE 1	[praʊd]	stolz
pull MORE 1	[pʊl]	ziehen
pumpkin U4/1	['pʌmpkɪn]	Kürbis
purple MORE 1	['pɜ:pl]	violett, lila
push U9/12	[pʊʃ]	schieben, drücken
push MORE 1	[pʊʃ]	schieben
put MORE 1	[pʊt]	setzen, legen, stellen
put on U6/6	[pʊt ɒn]	anziehen
put out U13/5	[pʊt aʊt]	löschen
pyjamas (no pl) U17/11	[pə'dʒɑ:məz]	Pyjama, Schlafanzug
pyramid U11/1	['pɪrəmɪd]	Pyramide

Q

quarter MORE 1	['kwɔ:tə]	Viertel(stunde)
queen U16/2	[kwi:n]	Königin
quiet MORE 1	['kwaɪət]	leise, ruhig
quite MORE 1	[kwaɪt]	ziemlich

R

race U16/6; U18/10	[reɪs]	rennen, rasen; Rennen
racing car U16/4	['reɪsɪŋ kɑ:]	Rennwagen
radio mast U18/9	[reɪdɪəʊ mɑ:st]	Sendemast
radiator U14/3	['reɪdieɪtə]	Heizkörper
raider U16/F	['reɪdə]	Räuber
railway U6/2	['reɪlweɪ]	Gleise, Schienen; (Eisen)bahn
rain MORE 1	[reɪn]	Regen; regnen
raincoat U19/5	['reɪnkəʊt]	Regenmantel
rainfall U19/8	['reɪnfɔ:l]	Niederschlag
rainforest U15/9	['reɪnfɒrɪst]	Regenwald
rainy U19/8	['reɪni]	regnerisch
rattle U13/1	['rætl]	klappern, rasseln
react U2/2	[ri'ækt]	reagieren
ready U5/NYC1	[redi]	fertig, bereit
reason U7/E3	['ri:zn]	Grund
recipe U10/7	['resəpi]	Rezept
record U2/5	['rekɔ:d]	Rekord
record U19/8	[rɪ'kɔ:d]	aufzeichnen
reddish U10/NYC2	['redɪʃ]	rötlich
refugee camp U12/7	[refjʊ'dʒi: kæmp]	Flüchtlingslager
religion U11/2	[rɪ'lɪdʒən]	Religion
repeat U11/9	[rɪ'pi:t]	wiederholen
report U19/4	[rɪ'pɔ:t]	Bericht
reporter U2/5	[rɪ'pɔ:tə]	Reporter/in
rerun U13/8	[ri:'rʌn]	Wiederholung
rescue MORE 1	['reskju:]	Rettung; retten
rest U18/8	[rest]	Rest; Ruhe
result U20/3	[rɪ'zʌlt]	Folge; Ergebnis
reward U20/NYC4	[rɪwɔ:d]	Belohnung

rhino (=rhinoceros) U5/10	['raɪnəʊ]	Nashorn, Rhinozeros
rhyme MORE I	[raɪm]	Reim
rice pudding U10/1	[raɪs 'pʊdɪŋ]	Milchreis
rich MORE I	[rɪtʃ]	reich
right-hand U7/2	['raɪthænd]	rechte(r, s)
Right here. U20/NYC4	[raɪt hɪə]	Hab' ich hier.
right now U13/8	[raɪt naʊ]	jetzt gerade
ring U5/NYC1	[rɪŋ]	anrufen
rise U19/4	[raɪz]	steigen
roast U13/6	[rəʊst]	rösten
roast potato U13/5	[rəʊst pə'teɪtəʊ]	Ofenkartoffel
role U16/2	[rəʊl]	Rolle
roller-skate U12/4	['rəʊləskeɪt]	Rollerblade fahren
Roman U7/7	['rəʊmən]	römisch
roof MORE I	[ru:f]	Dach
rope U2/E1	[rəʊp]	Seil
rotten U13/6	['rɒtən]	verfault, verdorben
round U6/4L;U9/5	[raʊnd]	um ... herum; rund
rub MORE I	[rʌb]	reiben
rubbish U8/7	['rʌbɪʃ]	Müll
rug U14/3	[rʌg]	Teppich
rule MORE I	[ru:l]	Regel; beherrschen
rusty U13/1	['rʌsti]	rostig

S

sacred U11/2	['seɪkrəd]	heilig
safe U5/1	[seɪf]	sicher
sail U18/10	['seɪl]	Segeln
salad U10/12	['sæləd]	Salat
salt U10/10	[sɔ:lt]	Salz
salt cellar U10/10	['sɒlt selə]	Salzstreuer
the same MORE I	[ðə 'seɪm]	der-/die-/dasselbe
sandal U11/3	['sændl]	Sandale
sausage U10/4	['sɒsɪdʒ]	Wurst, Würstchen
save MORE I	[seɪv]	retten
scale U19/1	[skeɪl]	Skala, Maßstab
scare MORE I	[skeə]	Angst machen, erschrecken
be scared MORE I	[bi: 'skeəd]	Angst haben
scary MORE I	['skeəri]	furchterregend; unheimlich
scene U2/2	[si:n]	Szene
science MORE I	['saɪəns]	Naturwissenschaft
scientist U11/12	['saɪəntɪst]	Wissenschaftler/in
scoop U10/9	[sku:p]	Kugel (Eiscreme)
scooter MORE I	['sku:tə]	Roller
score U15/G; U18/8	[skɔ:]	erreichen, erzielen (Tore); Punktestand, Spielstand
Scotland U1/2	['skɒtlənd]	Schottland
scream U13/1	[skri:m]	schreien; kreischen
screen U3/1	[skri:n]	Leinwand; Bildschirm
sculptor U20/1	['skʌlptə]	Bildhauer;
sculpture U3/2	['skʌlptʃə]	Bildhauerei; Skulptur, Plastik
sea MORE I	[si:]	Meer
sea level U19/8	[si: 'level]	Meeresspiegel
seat U2/2	[si:t]	(Sitz)platz
second U11/12	['sekənd]	Sekunde
secret U2/2	['si:krət]	geheim; Geheimnis
security U2/2	[sɪ'kjʊərəti]	Sicherheit
seed U9/5	[si:d]	Same(n)
seem U10/NYC2	[si:m]	scheinen
sell U11/3	[sel]	verkaufen
sergeant U2/2	['sɑ:dʒənt]	Sergeant; hier: Polizeimeister
series U3/7	['sɪəri:z]	Serie,; Reihe
serious U16/2	['sɪəriəs]	ernst
servant MORE I	['sɜ:vənt]	Diener/in
service U16/2	['sɜ:vɪs]	Service
set in U16/1	[set ɪn]	spielt in
several U7/7	['sevərəl]	einige, mehrere
shake U1/12	[ʃeɪk]	schütteln
That's a shame. U15/5	[ðæts ə 'ʃeɪm]	Wie schade! So ein Jammer!
shape MORE I	[ʃeɪp]	Form
share U14/7	[ʃeə]	teilen
shed MORE I	[ʃed]	Schuppen, Stall
sheep (pl sheep) U11/3	[ʃi:p]	Schaf
shell U1/7	[ʃel]	Schale; Muschel
shine U4/2	[ʃaɪn]	scheinen
shock U2/2	[ʃɒk]	Schock
shocked U11/14	[ʃɒkt]	schockiert, entsetzt
shooting U16/4	[ʃu:t]	Erschießung
shopping centre U6/G	['ʃɒpɪŋ 'sentə]	Einkaufszentrum
should U4/4	[ʃʊd]	sollte
shower U19/7	[ʃaʊə]	Regenschauer
shut U4/7	[ʃʌt]	schließen, zumachen
sick U15/9	[sɪk]	krank
feel sick MORE I	[fi:l 'sɪk]	sich schlecht fühlen
side U4/4	[saɪd]	Seite
sight U1/12	[saɪt]	Anblick
sign U6/3	[saɪn]	Zeichen, Schild
similar U3/8	[sɪmələ]	ähnlich
simple U12/3	['sɪmpl]	einfach
Singapore U2/2	[sɪŋə'pɔ:]	Singapur
single parent U12/7	['sɪŋgl 'peərənt]	Alleinerziehende/r
sink U14/3	[sɪŋk]	Spüle, Spülbecken
situation U19/7	[sɪtʃu'eɪʃn]	Situation, Lage
size U1/9	[saɪz]	Größe
skate U18/1	[skeɪt]	Rollschuh fahren, Rollerskate fahren
skill U16/4	[skɪl]	Geschick, Fähigkeit, Fertigkeit
sky U9/5	[skaɪ]	Himmel
slap somebody MORE I	['slæp sʌmbədi]	jemanden schlagen, jemandem einen Klaps geben
slave U11/3	[sleɪv]	Sklave/Sklavin
sleep U9/12	[sli:p]	Schlaf
slice U10/3	[slaɪs]	Scheibe

smart U20/3	[smɑ:t]	schlau
smell U11/3	[smel]	riechen
smile U5/14	[smaɪl]	Lächeln
snack U7/7	[snæk]	Snack, Imbiss
sneeze MORE 1	[sni:z]	niesen
sniff U7/F	[snɪf]	riechen, schnuppern
snow U19/2	[snəʊ]	Schnee
so-called U7/7	[səʊ'kɔ:ld]	sogenannt
So what? U1/7	[səʊ 'wɒt]	Na und?
solar panel U14/1	['səʊlə 'pænl]	Sonnenkollektor
soldier U11/8	['səʊldʒə]	Soldat/in
solo U18/10	['səʊləʊ]	Solo-
solve U2/2	[sɒlv]	lösen
somebody MORE 1	['sʌmbədi]	jemand
someone U7/E3	['sʌmwən]	jemand
something MORE 1	['sʌmθɪŋ]	etwas
sometimes MORE 1	['sʌmtaɪmz]	manchmal
somewhere U1/7	['sʌmweər]	irgendwo
son MORE 1	[sʌn]	Sohn
soon MORE 1	[su:n]	bald
sort MORE 1	[sɔ:t]	Sorte, Art
south U5/9	[saʊθ]	südlich, Süd-; Süden
southern U18/10	['sʌðən]	südlich, Süd-
space U4/1	[speɪs]	Weltall
spaceship U9/3	['speɪsʃɪp]	Raumschiff
speech bubble U20/5	[spi:tʃ bʌbəl]	Sprechblase
speed U16/4	[spi:d]	Geschwindigkeit, Tempo
spell U19/3	[spel]	Periode, Zeitabschnitt
put a spell on sb U13/5	[pʊt ə 'spel ɒn]	verzaubern
spend MORE 1	[spend]	ausgeben (Geld); verbringen (Zeit)
sphinx U11/1	[sfɪŋks]	Sphinx
spill U3/1	[spɪl]	verschütten
spirit U11/8	['spɪrɪt]	Geist
sportsman (pl -men) U18/3	['spɔ:tsmən, spɔ:tsmən]	Sportler
sportswoman (pl -women) U18/3	[spɔ:tswʊmən]	Sportlerin
spot U20/1	[spɒt]	Fleck
sprinkle U13/5	[sprɪŋkl]	sprenkeln, sprengen
square U6/8	[skweə]	Quadrat, Platz
stable U17/9	['steɪbl]	Stall, Box
stage U2/1	[steɪdʒ]	Bühne
stain U13/1	[steɪn]	Fleck
stand up (for) MORE 1	[stænd 'ʌp]	sich einsetzen (für)
starter U10/7	['stɑ:tə]	Vorspeise
starting point U19/8	['stɒ:tiŋ pɔɪnt]	Ausgangspunkt
state U17/9	[steɪt]	Bundesstaat
station U2/2	['steɪʃn]	Bahnhof; Station
statue U18/9	['stætʃu:]	Statue, Standbild
stay (at) U6/6	[steɪ]	übernachten (bei)
stay up late MORE 1	[steɪ ʌp 'leɪt]	lang aufbleiben
steal U2/5	[sti:l]	stehlen
step U11/8	[step]	Stufe
stick MORE 1	[stɪk]	Stock; kleben
stiff U2/2	[stɪf]	steif
still U3/2	[stɪl]	(immer) noch, noch immer
stomach U15/2	['stʌmək]	Magen
straight ahead U6/1	[streɪt ə'hed]	genau vor, geradeaus
straight on U6/3	[streɪt ɑ:n]	geradeaus
straightaway U10/5	[streɪtə'weɪ]	sofort
strange MORE 1	[streɪndʒ]	sonderbar
stranger U3/1	['streɪndʒə]	Fremde/r
strawberry U10/1	['strɔ:bəri]	Erdbeere
on strike U8/7	[ɒn 'straɪk]	im Streik
stripe MORE 1	[straɪp]	Streifen
stroke U17/1	[strəʊk]	streicheln
strong MORE 1	[strɒŋ]	stark
strongest MORE 1	['strɒŋgəst]	stärkste(r,s)
get stuck U13/2	[get 'stʌk]	steckenbleiben
student U20/3	['stju:dnt]	Student/in, Studierende/r; Schüler/in
study U8/10	['stʌdi]	studieren; lernen
stuff (informal) U13/6	[stʌf]	Zeug
stupid U3/F	['stju:pɪd]	dumm, blöd
subject (school) U1/5	[sʌbdʒɪkt]	(Schul)fach
such U17/7	[sʌtʃ]	solche, r, s
suddenly MORE 1	['sʌdnli]	plötzlich, auf einmal
suggestion U4/8	[sədʒestʃn]	Vorschlag
summary U9/E4	[sʌməri]	Zusammen-fassung
sun U7/1	[sʌn]	Sonne
superglue U4/4	['su:pəglu:]	Superkleber
supermarket U6/2	['su:pəmɑ:kɪt]	Supermarkt
surf (the net) U12/9	[sɜ:f]	surfen (im Internet)
survey U1/4	[sɜ:veɪ]	Umfrage
sweep U9/5	[swi:p]	kehren, fegen
swimmer U5/1	['swɪmə]	Schwimmer/in
swimming trunks U19/7	['swɪmɪŋ trʌŋks]	Badehose
swing U2/2	[swɪŋ]	(hin- und her-) schwingen
Swiss U18/6	[swɪs]	schweizerisch; Schweizer/in
switch off U12/9	[swɪtʃ'ɒf]	abschalten

T

Taipan U5/9	['taɪpæn]	Taipan-Schlange
take off U9/3	[teɪk 'ɒf]	abnehmen; abheben, starten
take out MORE 1	[teɪk 'aʊt]	herausnehmen
take part U7/8	[teɪk pɒ:t]	teilnehmen
tale MORE 1	[teɪl]	Geschichte
tan U19/9	[tæn]	(Sonnen)bräune
task U5/16	[tɑ:sk]	Aufgabe
teach U13/2	[ti:tʃ]	unterrichten
teapot U3/5	['ti:pɒt]	Teekanne
tear MORE 1	[teə]	zerreißen
tear MORE 1	[tɪə]	Träne
telegram U11/10	['telɪgræm]	Telegramm
telescope U19/8	['telɪskəʊp]	Teleskop

television U14/6	['telɪvɪʒn]	Fernsehgerät
tell off U20/3	[tel 'ɒf]	ausschimpfen
temperature U19/1	['temprɪtʃə]	Temperatur
temple U11/1	['templ]	Tempel
term U20/3	[tɜ:m]	Semester; Schuljahresabschnitt
terror MORE 1	['terə]	schreckliche Angst
text message MORE 1	['tekst 'mesɪdʒ]	SMS
(more) than U5/9	[ðæn]	(mehr) als
thank God U16/2	[θæŋk gɒ:d]	Gott sei Dank
their MORE 1	[ðeə]	ihr(e)
theirs U14/7	[ðeəz]	ihr(e, es)
them MORE 1	[ðem]	sie, ihnen
these MORE 1	[ði:z]	diese
thick U19/3	[θɪk]	dick
thief (pl thieves) U2/2	[θi:f, θi:vz]	Dieb/in
thirsty MORE 1	['θɜ:sti]	durstig
throat U15/2		Hals
through U6/3	[θru:]	durch
throughout the year U19/8	[θru:'aʊt ðə 'jɪə]	im ganzen Jahr
throw MORE 1	[θrəʊ]	werfen
thunderstorm U19/2	['θʌndəstɔ:m]	Gewitter
tickle MORE 1	['tɪkl]	kitzeln
tidy U8/1	['taɪdi]	aufräumen
tight U1/12	[taɪt]	fest
till U12/8	[tɪl]	bis
timetable U1/6	['taɪmteɪbl]	Stundenplan
tin MORE 1	[tɪn]	Büchse, Dose
today MORE 1	[tə'deɪ]	heute
toe U15/5	[təʊ]	Zeh(e)
together MORE 1	[tə'geðə]	zusammen, gemeinsam
toilet U20/1	['tɔɪlət]	Toilette, Klo
tomb U11/1	[tu:m]	Grab, Gruft
tomorrow MORE 1	[tə'mɒrəʊ]	morgen
ton U5/9	[tʌn]	Tonne (1000 kg)
tongue MORE 1	[tʌŋ]	Zunge
tongue twister U11/9	[tʌŋ twɪstə]	Zungenbrecher
tonight MORE 1	[tə'naɪt]	heute Abend
too MORE 1	[tu:]	zu; auch
tooth (pl teeth) U5/14	[tu:θ, ti:θ]	Zahn
torch U11/12	[tɔ:tʃ]	Taschenlampe
total U18/9	['təʊtl]	gesamt; völlig
touch MORE 1	[tʌtʃ]	berühren
tourist U1/1	['tʊərɪst]	Tourist/in
towards MORE 1	[tə'wɔ:dz]	in Richtung, auf ... zu
towel U5/1	['taʊəl]	Handtuch
toy MORE 1	[tɔɪ]	Spielzeug
track U20/3	[træk]	Weg; Anlage
tradition U4/3	[trə'dɪʃn]	Tradition
trailer U14/1	['treɪlə]	Anhänger, Wohnwagen
train U18/6	['treɪn]	trainieren
train U19/5	['treɪn]	Zug
trainer U18/8	['treɪnə]	Turnschuh; Trainer/in
trampolining U18/F	['træmpə'li:nɪŋ]	Trampolinspringen
translate U12/7	['træns'leɪt]	übersetzen
trap U7E3	[træp]	fangen; in einer Falle
travel U9/4	['trævl]	reisen
tray U17/1	[treɪ]	Tablett
treasure MORE 1	['treʒə]	Schatz
treat U4/1	[tri:t]	Vergnügen, Belohnung
tree house U14/1	['tri: haʊs]	Baumhaus
trick or treat U4/1	['trɪk ə 'tri:t]	Süßes oder Saures (Frage beim Halloween-Umzug)
tricky U11/2	['trɪki]	betrügerisch; schwierig, kompliziert
trilogy U16/4	['trɪlədʒi]	Trilogie
trip MORE 1	[trɪp]	Ausflug, Reise
triplet U12/3	['trɪplət]	Drilling
(it's no) trouble U10/NYC2	[ɪts nəʊ trʌbl]	keine Ursache
get into trouble U8/10	[get'ɪntu:'trʌbl]	Ärger bekommen
truth MORE 1	[tru:θ]	Wahrheit
try MORE 1	[traɪ]	versuchen
tummy U5/14	['tʌmi]	Bauch
turkey U10/1	['tɜ:ki]	Truthahn, -henne
turn off MORE 1	[tɜ:n 'ɒf]	abschalten
turn on MORE 1	[tɜ:n 'ɒn]	einschalten
turn up/down U19/7	[tɜ:n 'ʌp]	aufdrehen; runter drehen
twin U4/4	[twɪn]	Zwilling, Zwillings-
type (of) U1/2	[taɪp]	Art; Typ; Sorte
tyre U14/1	['taɪə]	Reifen

U

UFO (=unidentified flying object) U9/2	[jʊ:ef'əʊ]	Ufo (unbekanntes Flugobjekt)
ugly U5/6	['ʌgli]	hässlich
uncle U3/1	['ʌŋkl]	Onkel
unconscious U9/E4	[ʌn'kɒnʃəs]	bewusstlos
underline U1/8	[ʌndəlaɪn]	unterstreichen
unfortunately U20/3	[ʌn'fɔ:tʃənətli]	unglücklicherweise
unfriendly U13/6	[ʌn'frendli]	unfreundlich
uniform U7/7	['ju:nɪfɔ:m]	Uniform
unit U7/7	['ju:nɪt]	Einheit
university U12/7	[ju:nɪ'vɜ:səti]	Universität
unpack U19/7	[ʌn'pæk]	auspacken
until U1/F	[ən'tɪl]	bis
unusual MORE 1	[ʌn'ju:ʒʊəl]	ungewöhnlich
upon MORE 1	[ə'pɒn]	auf, an
upstairs U3/2	[ʌp'steəz]	oben
up to U4/4	[ʌp tu:]	bis zu
usually MORE 1	['ju:ʒʊəli]	gewöhnlich, normalerweise

V

valley U7/1	['væli]	Tal
vampire U4/1	['væmpaɪə]	Vampir
vegetable MORE 1	['vedʒtəbl]	Gemüse
vet U17/1	[vet]	Tierarzt, Tierärztin
village MORE 1	['vɪlɪdʒ]	Dorf
virtual U16/1	['vɜ:tʃuəl]	virtuell
voice U11/14	[vɔɪs]	Stimme
volcano U10/7	[vɒl'keɪnəʊ]	Vulkan
volume U19/7	['vɒlju:m]	Volumen; Lautstärke

W

waiter/waitress U10/5	['weɪtə, 'weɪtrəs]	Bedienung, Kellner/in
wall U1/1	[wɔ:l]	Wand
wallet U2/1	['wɒlɪt]	Brieftasche
war U12/7	[wɔ:r]	Krieg
wardrobe U14/3	['wɔ:drəʊb]	Kleiderschrank
wash up U7/10	[wɒʃ 'ʌp]	abspülen, abwaschen
washing U3/4	['wɒʃɪŋ]	Wäsche
do the washing-up U2/2	['du: ðə wɒʃɪŋ 'ʌp]	abspülen
waste of time U18/8	[weɪst əv taɪm]	Zeitverschwendung
watch U2/E1	[wɒtʃ]	beobachten; zuschauen
watch out U15/1	[wɒtʃ aʊt]	aufpassen; Achtung!
watch TV MORE 1	[wɒtʃ ti:'vi:]	fernsehen
waterfall U7/3	['wɔ:təfɔ:l]	Wasserfall
water skiing U12/4	['wɔ:təskiŋ]	Wasserski fahren
wave MORE 1	[weɪv]	winken
give way U19/1	[gɪv 'weɪ]	ausweichen, Platz machen
wear MORE 1	[weə]	tragen
weather MORE 1	['weðə]	Wetter
weatherman U19/7	['weðəmæn]	Wettermann
weaver U11/3	['wi:və]	Weber/in
weigh U5/9	[weɪ]	wiegen
weird U16/2	[wɪəd]	merkwürdig, seltsam, komisch
western U19/8	['westən]	westlich
wet U19/8	[wet]	nass
whale U5/9	[weɪl]	Wal
whale shark U5/12	[weɪl ʃɒ:rk]	Walhai
What about ... MORE 1	[wɒt ə'baʊt]	Was ist mit ...?
What for? U20/NYC4	[wɒt fɔ:]	Warum?, Wofür?
What's going on? MORE 1	[wɒts gəʊɪŋ 'ɒn]	Was ist los?
What's the matter? MORE 1	[wɒts ðə 'mætə]	Was ist los?
What's up? U16/2	[wɒts 'ʌp]	Was ist los?
wherever U19/7	[weə'revə]	wo(hin) auch immer
which MORE 1	[wɪtʃ]	welche(r, s)
while U17/7	[waɪl]	während
Who cares? U15/NYC3	[hʊ keəs]	Na, und?
whole MORE 1	[həʊl]	ganz
whose U14/8	[hu:z]	wessen
wide U11/14	[waɪd]	weit
wife (pl wives) MORE 1	[waɪf, waɪvz]	Ehefrau
will U19/3	[wɪl]	werden
windsurfing U19/9	['wɪndsɜ:fɪŋ]	Windsurfen
windy U4/2	['wɪndi]	windig
wing U18/9	[wɪŋ]	Flügel
wipe MORE 1	[waɪp]	abwischen, abputzen
witch U4/1	[wɪtʃ]	Hexe
without U16/3	[wɪð'aʊt]	ohne
witness U2/6	['wɪtnəs]	Zeuge, Zeugin
wizard U16/3	['wɪzəd]	Zauberer, Hexenmeister
wolf (pl wolves) MORE 1	[wʊlf, wʊlvz]	Wolf
woman (pl women) U13/2	['wʊmən, 'wɪmɪn]	Frau
(no) wonder U7/7	['wʌndə]	(kein) Wunder
wood MORE 1	[wʊd]	Wald, Holz
wooden MORE 1	['wʊdn]	Holz-, hölzern
wool U11/3	['wʊl]	Wolle
work U2/2; U9/5	[wɜ:k]	arbeiten; funktionieren; Arbeit
work out U12/4	['wɜ:k aʊt]	ausrechnen; hier: trainieren
worker U11/3	['wɜ:kə]	Arbeiter/in
workman (pl workmen) U11/10	['wɜ:kmən]	Handwerker
worldwide U5/9	[wɜ:ld'waɪd]	weltweit
be worried U8/9	[bi 'wʌrɪd]	sich Sorgen machen
be worth U18/9	[bi 'wɜ:θ]	wert sein
wound U11/10	[wu:nd]	Wunde

Y

yacht U18/10	[jɒt]	Jacht
yachtswoman U18/10	['jɒtswʊmən]	Jachtbesitzerin, Seglerin
not yet U16/6	[nɒt 'jet]	noch nicht
yours U14/7	[jɔ:z]	deine (r, s), Ihre (r, s)
youth MORE 1	[ju:θ]	Jugend

IRREGULAR VERBS

be	*was/were*	*been*	sein (war/waren) (MORE I)
become	*became*	*become*	werden (MORE I)
begin	*began*	*begun*	beginnen (MORE I)
blow	*blew*	*blown*	blasen
break	*broke*	*broken*	brechen (MORE I)
bring	*brought*	*brought*	bringen
build	*built*	*built*	bauen
buy	*bought*	*bought*	kaufen (MORE I)
catch	*caught*	*caught*	fangen (MORE I)
choose	*chose*	*chosen*	(aus)wählen (MORE I)
come	*came*	*come*	kommen (MORE I)
cut	*cut*	*cut*	schneiden (MORE I)
dig	*dug*	*dug*	graben (MORE I)
do	*did*	*done*	tun, machen (MORE I)
draw	*drew*	*drawn*	zeichnen (MORE I)
dream	*dreamt (dreamed)*	*dreamt (dreamed)*	träumen
drink	*drank*	*drunk*	trinken (MORE I)
drive	*drove*	*driven*	fahren, treiben (MORE I)
eat	*ate*	*eaten*	essen (MORE I)
fall (asleep)	*fell (asleep)*	*fallen (asleep)*	fallen (MORE I)
feel	*felt*	*felt*	fühlen (MORE I)
fight	*fought*	*fought*	kämpfen
find	*found*	*found*	finden (MORE I)
fly	*flew*	*flown*	fliegen (MORE I)
forget	*forgot*	*forgotten*	vergessen
hide	*hid*	*hidden*	(sich) verstecken (MORE I)
hurt	*hurt*	*hurt*	(sich) verletzen, schmerzen (MORE I)
get	*got*	*got*	bekommen, werden (MORE I)
get up	*got up*	*got up*	aufstehen (MORE I)
give	*gave*	*given*	geben (MORE I)
go	*went*	*gone*	gehen, fahren (MORE I)
hang	*hung*	*hung*	hängen (MORE I)
have	*had*	*had*	haben (MORE I)
hear	*heard*	*heard*	hören (MORE I)
hit	*hit*	*hit*	schlagen (MORE I)
hold	*held*	*held*	(fest)halten (MORE I)
know	*knew*	*known*	wissen, kennen (MORE I)
lay	*laid*	*laid*	legen (MORE I)
learn	*learnt (learned)*	*learnt (learned)*	lernen (MORE I)
leave	*left*	*left*	verlassen (MORE I)
let	*let*	*let*	lassen (MORE I)
lie	*lay*	*lain*	liegen (MORE I)
lose	*lost*	*lost*	verlieren
make	*made*	*made*	machen (MORE I)
meet	*met*	*met*	treffen (MORE I)
put	*put*	*put*	geben, setzen, stellen (MORE I)
read	*read*	*read*	lesen (MORE I)
ride	*rode*	*ridden*	reiten, fahren (MORE I)
ring	*rang*	*rung*	läuten (MORE I)
run	*ran*	*run*	laufen (MORE I)
say	*said*	*said*	sagen (MORE I)
see	*saw*	*seen*	sehen (MORE I)
send	*sent*	*sent*	senden, schicken (MORE I)
shoot	*shot*	*shot*	schießen
show	*showed*	*shown (showed)*	zeigen (MORE I)
sing	*sang*	*sung*	singen (MORE I)
sink	*sank (sunk)*	*sunk*	untergehen, sinken
sit	*sat*	*sat*	sitzen, sich setzen (MORE I)
sleep	*slept*	*slept*	schlafen (MORE I)
smell	*smelt (smelled)*	*smelt (smelled)*	riechen
speak	*spoke*	*spoken*	sprechen, sagen (MORE I)
spend	*spent*	*spent*	verbringen, ausgeben (MORE I)
stand	*stood*	*stood*	stehen (MORE I)
steal	*stole*	*stolen*	stehlen
swim	*swam*	*swum*	schwimmen (MORE I)
take off	*took off*	*taken off*	ausziehen (MORE I)
take	*took*	*taken*	nehmen (MORE I)
teach	*taught*	*taught*	lehren, unterrichten
tell	*told*	*told*	sagen, erzählen (MORE I)
think	*thought*	*thought*	denken (MORE I)
wake (up)	*woke (up)*	*woken (up)*	(auf)wachen (MORE I)
win	*won*	*won*	gewinnen (MORE I)
write	*wrote*	*written*	schreiben (MORE I)

CLASSROOM LANGUAGE

Can you understand your teacher?

We have plenty of time.
Have a go.
Have a guess.
Don't worry about your pronunciation.
Don't worry, it'll get better.
Maybe this will help you.
Can anybody correct this sentence?
That's very good.
Well done.
That's nice.
I like that.
You did a great job.
That's correct.
That's quite right.
Yes, you've got it.
That's much better.
That's a lot better.
You didn't make a single mistake.
Your pronunciation is very good.
You're getting better all the time.
Work in pairs/threes/fours/fives.
Work in groups of two/three/four.
Stand up and find another partner.
Have you finished?
Do the next activity.
Let's check the answers.
Come out and write it on the board.
Repeat after me.
Again, please.
Would you like to answer question 3?
Right. Now we will go on to the next exercise.
Have you finished?
Next one, please.
You have ten minutes to do this.
Your time is up.
Are you ready?
Any questions?
I'm afraid it's time to finish now.
We'll have to stop here.
Hang on a moment.
Just a moment, please.
One more thing before you go.
This is your homework.
Do exercise 9 on page 18 for your homework.
There is no homework today.

When you have a problem, say this:

Sorry? / Pardon?
Can you help me, please?
What's … in English, please?
I don't understand this.
Sorry, I've forgotten my …
Sorry, what's our homework?

ENGLISH SOUNDS

[ɑ:] **ar**m

[ʌ] f**u**n

[e] d**e**sk

[ə] **a**, an

[ɜ:] g**ir**l, b**ir**d

[æ] **a**pple

[ɪ] **i**n, **i**t

[i] ever**y**

[i:] **ea**sy, **ea**t

[ɒ:] **o**range, s**o**rry

[ɔ:] **a**ll, c**a**ll

[ʊ] l**oo**k

[u] Febr**u**ary

[u:] f**oo**d

[aɪ] **eye**, b**uy**

[aʊ] **ou**r

[eə] th**ere**

[eɪ] t**a**ke, th**ey**

[ɪə] h**ere**

[ɔɪ] b**oy**

[əʊ] g**o**, **o**ld

[ʊə] y**ou‘re**

[b] **b**ag, club

[d] **d**uck, car**d**

[f] **f**ish, lau**gh**

[g] **g**et, do**g**

[h] **h**ot

[j] **y**ou

[k] **c**an, du**ck**

[l] **l**ot, sma**ll**

[m] **m**ore, **m**u**m**

[n] **n**ow, su**n**

[ŋ] so**ng**, lo**ng**

[p] **p**resent, to**p**

[r] **r**ed, **r**ight

[s] **s**i**s**ter, cla**ss**

[t] **t**ime,ca**t**

[z] no**s**e, dog**s**

[ʒ] televi**si**on

[dʒ] oran**ge**

[ʃ] **s**ure, Engli**sh**

[tʃ] **ch**ild, **ch**eese

[ð] **th**ese, mo**th**er

[θ] **th**ink, mou**th**

[v] **v**ery, ha**v**e

[w] **wh**at, **w**ord

Acknowledgements

The publishers would like to thank the following for their kind permission to reproduce the following photographs and other copyright material:

AIP Emilio Segre Visual Archives, Lande Collection p85; **Alamy** p9, p35, p36, p38, p66 (CD: Food Icons), p72, p79, p82, p83 (playing basketball; playing tennis; shopping), p84 (Amar), p94, p103, p106, p113 (girl), p116, p122, p123 (mountain climbing), p130, p132 (cottage), p135, p140; **Boehmer Family** p83; **Corbis** p12 (blue ring octopus), p35 (taipan snake), p36 (elephant), p82 (grandfather; grandmother), p120 (injured horse), p134; **Fotolia** ©wuchen p97 (book); Gergely Fülüp p35 (bat); **Getty Images** p79 (Howard Carter); **Helbling** p9 (cd); p49; **©iStockphoto.com**/PaoloFrangiolli /GlobalP /syagci p9 steklon/ p12 /aldomurillo /creatives p32 / GlobalP /syagci /mikheewnik /viki2win /Laures p33 /Roseburn p35 (ostrich) / JJMaree/p36 /njmcc /aabejon p49 /Spanishalex /tepic / andipantz / MrPants p83 (swimming; tree climbing; reading; dancing) /fotoVoyager p94 (bungalow) /GordonsLife /Vasca /EuToch /Aeolos p97 /Gewitterkind p104 /pkline p106 (math quiz) /rgbspace / Andrew_Howe /Joe_Potato p116 (dry your pet; feed your pet; take your pet to the vet) /wsfurlan /cscredon p120 /Elerium /buzbuzzer / pamspix p122 (surfing; ice skating; windsurfing) /designsimply p123 (girl with surf board); **Shutterstock** Junial Enterprises p19, Jaren Jai Wicklund p23, Suzanne Tucker, Lisa Eastman p36 (boys), Galina Barskaya p46, Tony Campbell p47, Jaren Jai Wicklund p53, Elena Elisseeva, Simone van den Berg p59, Margita, Lee Torrens, Petr Vaclavek, Gerald Bernard, Peter Jochems; Maceofoto (peaches; cheesecake; plums; pumpkin pie; potatoes; rice pudding) p66, Pattie Steib p70, iofoto, Thomas M Perkins p82 (mother; aunt), KSR, Killroy Productions, Teresa Levite p84, Ulrike Hammerich, Juriah Mosin, iofotop 113, Tracy Whiteside p114, Aga & Miko Materne (arsat) p121, (skateboarder) p122, Kathy Burns-Millyard p124, Mikolaj Tomczak p127, Tracy Whiteside p128, Elena Elisseeva p132 (girl on beach); **User Wolfgangbeyer on de.wikipedia** p132 (Zabriskie Point, Death Valley); **Reuters** p126; **www.felixbaumgartner.com** W. Luif (portrait), B. Spoettl (base jumping) p125.

Commissioned Photography & Production by David Tolley Ltd. p 83 (girl on the phone); Studio Antonietti p101, p116

Every effort has been made to trace the owners of any copyright material in this book. If notified, the publisher will be pleased to rectify any errors or omissions.